Praise for *Loveable*

"Raw and liberating—the permission slip we all need to shed the conditioning that keeps us stuck."

—Jillian Turecki, *New York Times*
bestselling author of *It Begins with You*

"Some books you can't put down because the story is that good. Others wake you up to the person you're meant to become. In *Loveable*, Amber Rae accomplishes both. This book is a revelation—raw, transformative, and deeply inspiring."

—Terri Cole, psychotherapist
and author of *Too Much*

"A riveting story that will nudge you closer to standing in your truth. If you are looking for encouragement to change, love deeply, and choose emotional liberation, this book is for you."

—Alex Elle, *New York Times*
bestselling author of *How We Heal*

"Amber Rae's *Loveable* is more than a book—it's a master guide on liberation. For women everywhere who are afraid to live their most authentic, bravest, heart-led lives, consider these pages your invitation and your homecoming." —Jessica Zweig, bestselling author of *The Light Work*

"*Loveable* is a powerful blend of memoir and guidebook that will captivate you from the very first page. With raw vulnerability and unflinching honesty, Rae takes readers on a transformative journey of self-discovery and courage. . . . *Loveable* will leave you feeling seen, validated, and ready to step boldly into your most courageous life." —Vienna Pharaon, bestselling author of *The Origins of You*

"One of the most honest books I've ever read about learning to love yourself out loud." —Yasmine Cheyenne, author of *The Sugar Jar* and *Wisdom of the Path*

Also by Amber Rae

*The Feelings Journal: Find Your Way Through
Your Emotions*

*The Answers Are Within You: 108 Keys to Unlock
Your Mind, Body & Soul*

*Choose Wonder Over Worry: Move Beyond Fear
and Doubt to Unlock Your Full Potential*

LOVEABLE

One Woman's Path from Good to Free

Amber Rae

ST. MARTIN'S
ESSENTIALS
NEW YORK

First published in the United States by St. Martin's Essentials, an imprint of St. Martin's Publishing Group

EU Representative: Macmillan Publishers Ireland Ltd, 1st Floor, The Liffey Trust Centre, 117–126 Sheriff Street Upper, Dublin 1, D01 YC43

www.stmartins.com

The Library of Congress Cataloging-in-Publication Data is available upon request.

ISBN 978-1-250-80933-9 (hardcover)
ISBN 978-1-250-80934-6 (ebook)

Our books may be purchased in bulk for specialty retail/wholesale, literacy, corporate/premium, educational, and subscription box use. Please contact MacmillanSpecialMarkets@macmillan.com.

First Edition: 2025

10 9 8 7 6 5 4 3 2 1

For my husband, who gave me the courage
to rewrite my story.
And for my son—I lived this story
so you could live yours.

You do not have to be good.
You do not have to walk on your knees
for a hundred miles through the desert repenting.
You only have to let the soft animal of your body
love what it loves.

—*Mary Oliver*

Contents

Contents

Part 2: Be Brave

Contents

Part 3: Be Free

Contents

Author's Note

THE WORD *MEMOIR* COMES FROM THE FRENCH *mémoire,* meaning memory—a remembrance, a tracing of what was. But memory is not a perfect record. It is both a mirror and a mosaic—it reflects, but it also rearranges. It softens some edges and sharpens others. It forgets in order to protect, and it remembers in ways we don't always understand.

This book isn't the whole story—it's my story.

I have drawn from my journals, text messages, conversations, and my own recollection to piece together what I lived and how I made sense of it. Some moments remain vivid, preserved in ink and time-stamped messages. Others live in feeling rather than fact, in the imprint they left on me.

This book is not a chronicle of every detail, nor is it meant to be. It is an honest telling of what shaped me—the moments that cracked me open, the beliefs I carried, the truths I ran from and eventually turned toward. The truths that, in the end, set me free.

Prologue

The Miracle

I'M EIGHT YEARS OLD, HOLDING MY MOM AND grandma's hands as we walk into the hospital where my dad lives. I don't remember ever meeting my dad—he got into a bad car accident when I was three. He left my mom and me before that to "follow his dreams," but from the whisperings I hear, it sounds like all he did was cause trouble. Mom tells me his friend died in the crash, but my dad survived. Well, kind of. His brain is injured and he can't really move or talk or anything.

But that doesn't stop me from thinking about him. I wonder what he's like and if I'm like him. I wonder if he'd like spending time with me. When I see my friends with their dads, I study them closely and imagine what it would be like to have one too. I picture him reading me books, holding my hand, singing to me. My mom says nice things about him, like "He loved you very much" and "You're really smart—just like him," but I can tell it hurts her to talk about him. It makes me wonder why he left us—why he left *me*.

I tried on a lot of outfits this morning, hoping to find the right thing to wear. I didn't let my mom or grandma help because I like to do it myself. I picked out my favorite jean jumper and black patent leather shoes. They're shiny and they make me feel pretty. I hope my dad likes them.

As we walk through the hospital, I feel a fluttering in my stomach, kind of like when I'm on a roller coaster. It smells funny here, like microwave food and bleach. My mom and grandma tell me if I want to leave at any point, all I have to do is squeeze one of their hands and we'll go.

When we walk into his room, I see my dad lying in a bed, hooked up to a bunch of machines. His face is swollen, and he doesn't really look like his pictures. But he smiles when he sees me, and his eyes follow me around the room. This makes me feel special. I see photos of me on a bulletin board near his bed, and it makes me smile big. I wonder how they got there and if he knows who I am.

I walk up closer to him and say, "I'm Amber."

"Ambah," he says slowly, barely able to get the words out. But I don't care. He just said my name!

"She's Beverly," I say, pointing to my mom.

"Beberly," he says.

"And that's Kate," I say, pointing to my grandma.

"Kade," he says.

"I luuvv you," he says to me in that same silly way, smiling big, making me gasp and feel all warm inside, like I've been waiting forever to hear those words. I now know that I do have a dad, and he knows my name, and he loves me.

"I luuvv you," he says again, this time looking at my mom, which makes me laugh but also makes my belly feel weird. I thought those words were just for me. "I luuvv you," he says again, this time to the nurse as she walks through the door.

Wait . . . what? I look at my dad and then at the nurse, my pulse speeding up.

"Oh, he's our lover here," the nurse says. "He tells everyone, *I love you, I love you.* He doesn't stop saying it." *Oh*, I think as I look down at my shoes, which I don't think he noticed. My nose starts to burn in the way it does when I'm about to cry. I feel my mom and grandma looking at me, so I tell myself to be a good, strong girl, and then I look up quickly and smile like everything is just fine.

"Amber," I say to my dad again.

"Ambah," he says back. We play the name game for what feels like a long time. I try to teach him other words, but I like when he says my name best, and I just want to keep hearing him say it.

When the visiting hours are over, the nurse wheels my dad's bed into the other room and we follow. "Wait," I say to my mom and grandma, just outside his room. I run back in, take one last look around, and pin my latest school photo to his bulletin board. *Maybe he'll remember me this way*, I think.

I leave the room and wave goodbye to my dad. He smiles at me, and the nurses wave too. When we get to the car, I say quietly from the back seat, "I don't want to come back here again." My mom says "Okay," and we drive away.

⇒·⇐

LATER THAT WEEK I'M sitting on swings with my friends at recess. Laughter fills the air, the swings creaking out a melody.

"I met my dad a few days ago," I tell them. "And get this: When I walked into the room, he said my name. Even though he has a brain injury and he shouldn't be able to do that, he somehow knew it was me, and he was able to say Amber."

"Wow," my friends say. "That's so cool."

"Yeah," I say. "And then he told me he loved me. He just kept saying, "I love you, I love you, I love you." The nurses couldn't believe it, because it was the first time he'd said that to anyone. They said it was a miracle."

I say *miracle* with so much conviction that my friends open their mouths and look at me with wide eyes of amazement. We all kick our feet, swinging higher and higher toward the sky.

⇒-⇐

I'M THIRTY-TWO YEARS OLD, sitting on a couch in my fiancé's family's apartment. We've been engaged for seven years, and we finally have plans to tie the knot. I can feel the relief in the room when we talk about the wedding. It's as if everyone's exhales all say the same thing: *At last.* I get it; I'm exhaling too. I've gone back and forth on this decision so many times, I can barely see straight. *Am I happy here? Is he my person? He's a good man and we have a good life—shouldn't that be enough? Am I being ungrateful? Is it okay we don't have sex? Is it selfish of me to want more? Can I be happy here?*

But I've decided once and for all: I can make this work.

I tell his family the story of meeting my dad because I desperately need another miracle. Except this time, when I say the word *miracle*, a knot takes root in my stomach.

That's not what happened, a voice within me says.

I swat the voice away. *Of course that's what happened. I know my story.*

When I look around the room, I see the wide eyes and

4

open mouths I've come to expect. But I also notice my fiancé's cousin, an emergency room doctor, looking at me with eyes that say, *I don't believe you*. His look shakes me because it points to a more honest truth: I no longer believe me either.

I've wondered for some time what my little girl was really feeling, wishing I could go back and ask her, *Why did you make up that story?*

But now I know why:

That little girl wanted nothing more than to feel loved and cherished by her father—the one man incapable of giving her this. Instead his abandonment led her to believe she was the kind of girl unworthy of deep love and connection.

Eight-year-old Amber made up that story to protect herself, not knowing that just like my father was trapped in his body, confined to his hospital bed, that story would trap me there with him.

Little did I know, it would take another quarter century to free myself.

Part 1

Be Good

The Ceremony

SEVEN MONTHS AFTER SITTING IN MY FIANCÉ'S family's apartment, I'm in Morocco, standing on a custom-built circular platform, enveloped by flowers, at the base of the Atlas Mountains, with seventy friends and family members fencing us in. The light is perfect. The floral arrangements are perfect. The music is perfect. My dress, hair, and makeup are perfect. The two camels that helped us make a grand entrance are perfect. The pitch I emailed to *Vogue* to cover our wedding is . . . perfect.

But one thing is not perfect: I just walked down the aisle thinking, *I don't know how long this is going to last.*

The ceremony begins and I lean toward my soon-to-be husband and rub my nose against his. The crowd *ooh*s and *ahh*s as a belly laugh erupts through me, my head tilting back. I can't tell if I'm performing or being real, and I'm unsettled to not know the difference. The moment comes when it's time for me to say my vows.

What I say is this:

The first time your eyes locked with mine, it felt as if my soul was bringing me back to someone it had known for thousands of years.

What I think is this: *I don't feel close to you. You feel so far away. I can't reach you.*

What I say is this:

As I stand here today, in a circle of eternal love and unconditional commitment, I commit to choose you—all of you—until the last breath I take.

What I think is this: *I'm stuck. How will I ever make this work?*

And this:

I'm still mad that, two nights ago, on the first dinner of our wedding weekend, you were nowhere to be found. I finally discovered you hiding out in a room, where the Wi-Fi was strongest, on a business call. I don't know why this was so surprising to me; I should've known that's where you'd be. When I grabbed your phone and spoke sternly into the line, "My fiancé is not available. He's getting married this weekend," you laughed. You then proceeded to tell people this story all night, calling it "cute." It is not cute. I want to blow up this perfect circular platform I'm standing on. I want to tear apart the flower arrangements and rip off this ridiculously expensive dress and run away.

But that would be crazy. We love each other and I really do want this. I think.

So instead I smile and say my lines like an actor who knows her part. *They're so in love,* people probably think. *They're perfect together.*

What a performance. What a great *story.*

The Turquoise-Blue Box

MANY YEARS AGO, WHEN I WAS FEELING DIREC-tionless in my career, I listened to a guided visualization that promised to "help me find my gift for the world." I wasn't fully convinced this could actually help me, but I was lost, so I figured, *Why not?*

As I lay on my couch, eyes closed, a woman's voice guided me to imagine my ideal creative environment. I pictured myself sitting on the ground of an empty studio with floor-to-ceiling windows. "Look for the door in the room," the woman instructed. "Your gift for the world is on the other side."

I stood up eagerly, walked to the door, and swung it open, anxious to see what I'd find. I expected to see a stack of books but was instead surprised to find a young girl stand-ing there—*My future daughter? My inner child?*—with a small turquoise-blue box glowing in her hands. The girl placed the box in my open palms and whispered in my ear, "If you're ever lost, open this."

I closed the door, looked at the box expectantly, then

opened it. A ray of yellow light shot out into my heart and then out into the space. Suddenly the studio was alive with art, books, plants, and all the things I hoped to create one day. This girl and the turquoise box would continue to visit me from time to time in my visualizations and dreams—a signal, I interpreted, that I was "on the right track."

Years later my fiancé and I were leaving on a trip to Morocco when a friend dropped off a gift: a small strip of acid that came from a guy who supplies it to a famous rock band. "Put it in the back of one of your journals," he suggested. "No one will find it there." I'd never taken acid before, and traveling overseas with it seemed risky, but I slipped it into the pages of my journal anyway—just in case.

By the time we'd landed in Marrakech and trekked out to the remote hotel—a fortresslike building with rose-colored walls made of earth, olive groves, lush landscaping, and 360-degree views of the Ourika Valley, I knew we were in the perfect setting for a psychedelic trip. While my fiancé spent the first few hours staring at a doorknob, I was in the shower, watching art appear on the walls like a paint by numbers.

Suddenly a voice within me said: "The mountains are calling and we must go." We left our room and walked out onto the property, exploring hidden corners, the hotel's tranquil gardens, and rustic dirt pathways. As the story goes, my fiancé sprinted ahead as a turquoise box, nestled in the desert, came into view. He picked it up and shook it above his head, screaming, "THE MOTHERFUCKING TURQUOISE-BLUE BOX."

We had found the box from my visualization in real life.

"I don't know what's real or not real anymore," he said, awestruck.

A few years later, while we were wedding planning, when people would ask why we chose to get married in Morocco, we'd say something along the lines of: *We didn't choose Morocco; Morocco chose us. It was destined. A turquoise-blue box led us here. . . .*

And it's true—we did find a turquoise-blue box there.

And I did see that box—albeit a much smaller one—in visualizations and dreams.

And my fiancé did scream, "THE MOTHERFUCKING TURQUOISE-BLUE BOX!" while shaking it above his head.

And in that moment we were filled with awe and rapture and delight.

But we were also on drugs.

And . . .

The sliver of the story I conveniently left out is this: we didn't find the box nestled in the desert, like a lost treasure. We found it sitting on a table in a corner of the hotel.

"I don't know what's real or not real anymore."

What's real is this: We stole the motherfucking turquoise-blue box. Then I used it as a symbol to prove our love was real—meant to be. Even though my inner knowing was desperately trying to warn me that I'd chosen yet another man who could never give me the love and connection I so deeply desired, I still needed a sign to convince myself I was "on the right path."

And then we got married at the very site of our thievery.

Lies

A FEW MONTHS AFTER GETTING MARRIED, MY husband and I began working with a therapist to "deepen our bond" and "grow as a couple." At least that's what I told the therapist in our introductory email. She replied by noting that so many couples wait until they are in a dire situation to get help, but that did not seem to be the case with us. Her words made me queasy, but I also hoped she was right.

Now every time we have a call with her, we start by telling her what is going great in our relationship. It's as if we're sitting down with a friend over a glass of wine, eager to share with her our exciting life and work updates.

I got another book deal!

He has an exciting work development!

Everything is going great!

Forty-five minutes in and my husband is still talking about his meetings with investors and what this could mean for our future. I then jump in to share all the synchronicities that are pointing to our next life move. The hour ends and we've addressed nothing of substance. She reflects back excitement and encouragement and coins us "the couple she doesn't have to worry about."

I sit there quietly, wondering when I got so good at making other people think I'm fine.

On our next call, my husband kicks things off by saying, "Our relationship is at ninety-eight percent alignment right now. How do we get to one hundred percent?"

Does withholding from our therapist that we're not having sex and we're sleeping in separate bedrooms qualify as 98 percent alignment? Does ignoring the fact that I feel lonely and I don't want my husband to touch me and I'm not sure if I want to stay in this marriage mean there's only 2 percent of work to do? Doesn't avoiding all hard but important conversations indicate we are actually not in alignment at all?

But I don't say anything. I'm too scared to speak the truth. I like being the kind of person our therapist doesn't have to worry about. It's easier, and more comfortable, to pretend. By focusing my energy on making our life this grand, sweeping adventure—one I can share freely as inspiration to our friends and family, and my online community—I can distract myself from what's broken.

To tell the truth would mean admitting that I'm living a lie.

I Can Make This Work

SIX MONTHS LATER, I STILL FEEL EMOTIONALLY starved and we're still not having sex. And on the rare occasion we do, it's so I can check off an imaginary box. I fuck my husband twice a year to quiet the voice that whispers: *Something is wrong. Very wrong.* Many women feel shame around sex, pleasure, and desire, but it's usually about having it, not lacking it. Despite so much of our relationship that appears to be working on the surface, there's one shame-inducing truth I'm terrified to address: We've never had a real sexual relationship. And even more shameful, still: Neither one of us seems to care.

But one night a few glasses of pinot noir uncorks a repressed desire in me, and I'm lunging at my husband in the kitchen. I'm kissing and humping and rubbing him. I feel aroused for the first time in years. I don't care if it's just the alcohol, but feeling turned on is like that first ravenous breath of air, a desperate gasp, after being held underwater for too long. *Maybe nothing's wrong with me after all. Maybe we can make this work.*

My husband is half-heartedly kissing me back and touching me but barely opening his mouth. I try harder. But his lips remain tight. Suddenly he backs his face away, squeezes my shoulders, kisses my forehead, and walks into his office. I hear him sit down in his chair and open his laptop. There is no acknowledgment of the moment we've just shared. There is no "Hey, I gotta go do one work thing, but I'll meet you in the bedroom in five." He just walks away, leaving me stunned. I adjust my shirt and smooth out my hair, wondering what the hell just happened. I sit down on the couch, take a large gulp of wine, stroke my cat, and wait for his next move. But the only movements I hear are the sound of his fingers typing away on the keyboard.

Not willing to give up and still convinced I can make this work, I walk into his office and say with as much flirtation as I can muster, but with more frustration than I intend:

"You have two options tonight: you can wire into your work or you can make love to your wife."

I don't really want to have sex anymore, but I need to so I can alleviate my fear that our relationship is doomed. But his body only stiffens and his shoulders cave forward.

"I'm sorry, but I need to get ready for tomorrow," he says, glancing up at me quickly before returning to his screen.

I'm not sure if I should feel angry or relieved.

When I married my husband, it was my greatest hope that we would find our way and figure things out. With time and therapy, surely we'd get on the same page. The vision of what our love could be would finally match the reality of our relationship. I'd gaze into his eyes and *feel* him. I'd feel seen and loved and we'd have wild and intimate sex. But the only wild sex I was having happened in the recurring dreams about my ex. Rather than admit my unhappiness, I doubled down on the story of our love. I would push my way through instead of giving up. I would not be a quitter. I was stuck in the deep-seated belief of *I can make this work* rather than knowing when to let go.

When the pandemic hit, and we were now, for the first time in our relationship, stuck in the same space together—him pacing around the house, talking loudly on work calls all day; me hiding in the bedroom, trying to write—it was fertile soil for *I can make this work*. We found a ritual that turned into a habit: He cooked elaborate dinners each night and I stood in line at the local wine shop with a mask and gloves on, waiting eagerly to discover which bottle of wine would pair perfectly with what was on the menu. An earthy Gamay for lamb pasta; a high-acid Txakolina for whole branzino. Food and drink became our primary mode of connection and experiencing pleasure, which is another way of saying we didn't emotionally connect but numbed ourselves together.

When the sheen of this routine wore off, I came up with a new plan: Now that my husband wasn't tied to an office, we could finally leave New York. The city had been wearing on me for years, and we had talked for some time about finding a slower and less expensive pace. Two weeks and a few phone calls later we rented out our furnished Brooklyn apartment and got a tip from a friend to visit Todos Santos. He described it as "part artist's village, part desert oasis" near the sea in Baja, on the Tropic of Cancer. It felt dreamy, and our friend offered to rent us an open casita.

With two suitcases and two cats, we set out on a new adventure. I felt elated and relieved, certain this would be the Thing. The Thing that would solve our marital problems.

The Thing that would create happily ever after. The Thing that would save us. The Thing that would save me.

For the first few months we took long beach walks and sipped margaritas at sunset. We held hands and explored the coast. *I really can make this work*, I thought. *I can be his wife.* That new vacation glow masked our troubles at first, but it wasn't long before he was working even longer hours, I was back to criticizing his behavior, and my true feelings were surfacing yet again: *I can't reach him. He feels so far away. I'm so lonely. Can I really make this work?* But now was not the time to give up—I had come so far, and certainly there was a way to bring us closer together.

I'd always dreamt of collaborating with my husband on a project, and one day while walking along the beach, an inspired idea struck: What if we built a sanctuary by the sea for artists, creators, and innovators to retreat from the noise of modern life to work on their most meaningful projects? It was a hot market for buying and developing land, and we had just made this leap in our own lives, so I figured, *Why not?* While neither of us had a background in land development, my husband had built a sixty-thousand-square-foot start-up space for entrepreneurs in San Francisco, and I had spent years designing coaching programs to help people actualize their true potential.

When I shared this vision with him, he too was excited about taking the risk of figuring out a project of this scale. If I couldn't find closeness with him in our relationship, surely I'd be able to once he was my business partner. *This* would be the Thing. The Thing that would actually save us.

A few chance encounters later and we were closing on a

plot of land to build our family home, and we had stumbled on four perfect acres for the land project right across the road. It was all unfolding so effortlessly and seamlessly that I was sure this really was the Thing. All we needed to do next was raise the capital to make it happen.

When our two-year wedding anniversary rolled around, I managed—at last—to pull him from work for a one-night romantic getaway. The car was packed, our cat sitter was here, and I was wearing my flowy dress, sun hat, and flip-flops. My husband was pacing around the kitchen on a business call, speaking with such exuberance that the whole neighborhood could hear him. I walked inside, tapped my wrist, and with a firm tone, said, "We need to go *now*."

He put his pointer finger in the air to suggest *one more minute*, which I knew in reality meant ten. Probably twenty. Then he spun around, frazzled. I sighed, feeling dismissed. I walked outside, sat on the steps that looked out at the sea, the frustration of this moment a familiar friend. My cat Leo rubbed his body against mine, purring.

I looked out at the land in front of me—tropical flowers sprouting from sand, native cacti and succulents thriving in arid soil, and lush palm trees swaying in the coastal breeze. Wild horses fed on grass while birds chirped a sweet symphony. I hoped desperately that this plan would work—that I could make a home for myself here and this could be the place where our relationship would bloom. But even though everything looked serene on the surface, a gnawing uncertainty ached within.

My husband came running outside, heavy on the apologies and raring to go. We got in the car, made a "no phone" pact for the trip, and I took a long, deep breath.

Finally.

He had no idea where we were going—it was a surprise. I directed him to the fancy hotel I'd managed to get a last-minute deal on and we strolled in, immediately making our way to the pool bar.

Two spicy mezcal margaritas, please.

The day unfolded not as I had hoped, but as I had come to expect:

We sipped margaritas and talked business. We made new friends at the pool and talked business. We jumped in the sea and talked business. We had a romantic meal and . . . talked business.

In between bites of fish and sips of pinot noir, I jotted down strategies and next steps in my pocket-size notebook.

"Who else could we bring in as an investment partner?" he asked as I began rattling off possible names. "Ben can host events for his start-ups down here," he added. "It'd be silly for him not to invest. I'll give him a call next week."

"I don't want this to be focused on start-ups, though," I said. "It's more about mindfulness, going inward, and creating the things that move us. It's more creativity and less entrepreneurship. I want Ben to do his own deepest work here rather than just facilitate his clients' dreams."

"Mm-hmm, totally," he said, but I worried he did not mean. Just as the sun was setting, a band arrived at our table with romantic melodies in tow. I sat taller in my seat and looked at him beggingly, eager for a shift in tone. But I couldn't catch his eye. He was looking up at the sky—thinking. I caved back into my seat wondering if this was how the Thing that saves us was supposed to feel. Shouldn't the Thing bring us closer together rather than drive us further apart? *Maybe I can't make this work.*

We headed back to our hotel room at night's end, a bottle of champagne on ice to greet us, rose petals sprinkled on the bed. I popped the cork, poured two glasses, and slipped into bed. The mood was just right for intimacy, but we didn't have sex because sex was not something we did in our relationship. Instead we watched an episode of *The Voice* and my husband fell fast asleep.

As I lay in bed next to him, all I wanted was for him to turn toward me, place his hands on my face, look into my eyes, and say, "Thank you for planning this for us. I love you so much." But the voice I heard wasn't his; it was John Legend giving a standing ovation to a singer he'd just met. I yearned for even an ounce of that attention and affection.

I tried to sleep, but I sat wide-awake in bed instead, my mind spinning.

How did I get here? How have I found myself in a sexless relationship where my needs for closeness and emotional depth aren't met? Why have I let this be okay? Why do I keep holding on to hope that something will change, when nothing is changing? Why, when something feels off, when something feels missing, do I not listen? Why am I so afraid of disappointing others but so willing to disappoint myself? How did I of all people—a woman whose work is devoted to helping people live their most authentic and true lives—find myself here?

I had tried, with all of me, to not know these truths. I had made my life so busy and full—chasing experience after experience, delight after delight, New Thing after New Thing—anything to dull the loneliness and ache I felt inside. The wisdom I shared in my books and on stages had been words I spoke, not truths I fully lived—and now, this was my chance to put it into practice. To sit still and let myself feel and know and hear the burning truth within me:

I'm married to my best friend, who feels like a brother, not a romantic life partner. I will not find the Thing that saves us. I have to save myself.

Those words thundered inside my chest like lightning brewing on the horizon. But what was I supposed to do about this now? So many big plans were in motion; I couldn't possibly just walk away. The thought of blowing up my life, hurting the people I loved, and starting anew felt impossible. The only thing I could muster the courage to do was pour myself another glass of champagne and hope that clarity was coming. I pulled out my journal and wrote, *God, Goddess, Dad, ancestors, Universe, whoever is out there. Can I get some help—please?*

Hello Again

IF I HAD KNOWN HOW QUICKLY MY CRY FOR HELP would be answered, I'm not sure I would've had the guts to ask.

The next day, we're back home from our rendezvous—I'm unpacking in my bedroom while my husband is settling back into his across the hall. Six months ago I pointed to his loud snoring as the reason for needing my own room, but in truth, I could no longer bear the closeness when we were so emotionally far apart. Now back in our separate rooms, the weight of our failed attempt at reconnection feels heavier than ever. But still, I cling to the hope of what our relationship could be, rather than facing the truth of what it has become.

Before I have a chance to fully unpack the layers beneath our anniversary getaway, I realize the time. A couple is on their way to learn more about investing in our land project, a meeting I'd forgotten. I'm tempted to cancel, still dizzy from the night before. But it's too late. They're already on their way and they invited a friend to tag along.

As I freshen up, I think about what the next hour or so will look like: We'll give a pitch of what we're creating, a tour of the land, and then we'll see if they want to invest. That last part is my least favorite—selling our idea and trying to convince people to put their money into our project. It feels vulnerable to ask for help—especially when it's financial. The fear of asking for too much, of needing to depend on others, of losing creative control—it stirs up discomfort. But at least there's mezcal for courage.

I seem to forget all of this when our three guests, dressed like they just walked off a movie set, step out of the car. I can't tell if it's the way they move or how the sun is glistening on their skin at golden hour, but there is a slowing down to this moment that takes my breath away. I feel a gravitational pull toward them, but I can't put my finger on why.

I greet the woman with a hug, say hello to her partner, and turn last to a man whose hazel eyes suddenly bring time to an abrupt halt. My body leans toward him. My head tilts to the side.

"Hello, I'm John," he says.

I say, "Hello, John," but it feels like "Hello, again." A quiet calm blooms within me as I meet his gaze, like I'm returning home after a lifetime away. Whether the moment lasts for seconds or minutes or hours, I can't tell you. All I know is that something inside me shifts. My body turns slowly toward the house, though our eyes remain locked. I try to gather my composure, my steps leading us to the terrace ahead.

I guide them along a path lined with fuchsia bougainvillea and white jasmine in full bloom. Waves crash in the distance, adding salt to air already sweet. We walk down a few steps onto a patio facing the sea. My senses heighten, as if looking into John's eyes has jolted me awake from a deep sleep. Suddenly, the colors are more vivid, the ocean breeze lingers on my lips, and my skin prickles with electricity where we touched.

My husband is in the kitchen mixing cocktails, so the other man heads inside to help. There are two couches facing each other. I sit on one, while John and the woman sit across from me on the other.

I feel flushed and wired. There is so much energy pulsing through my body that I don't know what to do with myself. I stand up to tell them about the project and what led my husband and me to the land. I feel myself nervously floating around the space and talking excitedly with my arms. I'm at a loss for what to do with my hands, not to mention where to set my eyes.

John watches me steadily with a soft smile. I feel vulnerable and exposed, like he is seeing all of me. I like both his presence and his attention very much, and I am terrified by it. As I begin to say, "My husband and I have a dream to . . ." my voice cracks and then falls away, the end of the sentence hanging unfinished. All the while, John continues to smile, his attention steady and kind. I feel like I can't breathe.

What on earth is happening to me?

I sit down to catch my breath. My husband walks out with cocktails. *Dear god, thank you. Please make me stop talking. Please take the attention away from me. Please hand me a drink—now.*

We clink our glasses to celebrate new friendship, and I take a big gulp. John and I, like it's the most natural thing, choose two chairs side by side. As the other three drop into a conversation about business and investments, we slip easily into a conversation, just the two of us, together.

He's an artist; I'm a writer. His father passed away six years ago; mine, twenty-one. He's working on a new body of work; I'm writing my next book but I haven't cracked the big idea yet. I show him an illustration I just made that's in a new style named "The In-Between"; he suggests I use that as the working title for my book. He explains that he titles his creative works at the beginning of a project because it points him toward the essence of what he's creating, even when the destination is unclear. I like the way his mind works. He meditates daily; I journal. He feels a strong connection to birds; I to cats. His father visits as a ladybug; mine as a monarch butterfly. He's from New York; I've lived there most of my adult life. He's now in Venice, California—the place I've tried and failed to move to three times in the last three years.

It's not just our similarities that draw me in, though they're hard to ignore. What captivates me is John himself. There's a quiet confidence about him—the kind that comes from knowing yourself deeply—and it pulls me in like gravity. He's self-assured but not cocky, comfortable in his own skin. He's walked through grief, faced loss, and emerged grounded and steady, with a strength that feels earned. He also has this no-bullshit New Yorker quality about him that makes him refreshingly real. I don't have to guess what he's thinking or read between the lines; he speaks with a healthy balance of candor and kindness.

Their planned one-hour visit lasts five, and somewhere along the way, I realize something undeniable—my soul knows John's, and it's one of the most extraordinary I've ever met. I can't help but notice the contrast between how I feel in conversation with my husband and how I feel right now with John. Perhaps it's an unfair comparison, I know, but the thought lingers, and I'm unsettled by it. Suddenly I'm filled with a longing that I haven't known has been living inside me for years. I wonder for a brief moment what life would have been like had I met someone like him sooner. That vision electrifies me—and saddens me somehow too.

Two artists work on their craft side by side and make love under a moonlit . . .

But no. *No, no, no.*

I stop the fantasy midstream and decide we shall be eternal soul brother and sister instead. And so I blurt out in earnest:

"I'm going to match you with your person!"

As soon as the words leave my mouth, I feel my cheeks flush as I realize the absurd boldness of my statement. *Match you with your person* . . . Why on earth would I say such a thing? But then he looks at me, takes me in, and laughs. He *laughs*. Dear god, the sound of his laugh. The way his head tilts back as one eye squints slightly more than the other. The way his smile sends shock waves through my system. The spark he lights in me is undeniable, so I try to diffuse it.

"No, no, but really. I have a track record with this sort of thing. I have several married couples under my belt."

"I trust you do and really, that's a lovely offer," he says. "But honestly, I'm six weeks out of a relationship and just trying to focus on myself right now."

"Oh, I'm sorry to hear that."

"No, don't be. Our breakup was the last straw in a ten-year pattern of dating the same kind of woman who's not available. I've been doing the work around it for many years, but now I'm putting that final piece into place around genuinely loving myself and knowing that I'm okay no matter what.

That I don't need to convince someone to love me to know that I'm lovable."

His words ring so true that I let out an audible gasp. I can't help but wonder what will be my last straw. I'm tempted to lean in and tell him everything—how my relationship feels broken, how I don't know what to do—but instead I look him straight in the eye and say, "I understand more than you know and can relate deeply. 'I'm okay no matter what'— that's beautiful. I'm taking that with me."

"It's yours," he says with a soft smile. "And I'll be sure to let you know when I'm ready for love."

It's late now. It's time for them to go. But I don't want the night to end. I want to press pause on this moment and watch it on repeat forever. They stand to leave. We hug goodbye. We don't let go. I can feel my heart and his heart beating at once. Our bodies colliding and confiding in each other. Our souls remembering what it's like to feel this way. We pull back and I take one last look at the Universe inside his eyes.

As they walk away, into the moonlit sky, I turn to my husband and say without thinking, "I just met a soulmate."

"I saw," he says with a generous clarity that catches me off guard. "That was beautiful to witness."

Doorways

UH-OH WAS THE FIRST THING I THOUGHT THAT night lying in bed, followed quickly by *But that felt so good*. I didn't know what to do with all the desire, longing, and confusion coursing through me, so I did what the kids do these days—I posted about my feelings real-time to my Instagram story, making a nod to the "soul friend" I had just met, and how beautiful and unexpected life can be. *John?* our one mutual friend DMs me immediately. *How did she know?*

Even though I felt guilty doing so, I allowed myself to think about our spark a little longer—how he made me feel, how I'd never known a connection like that, when I might, if ever, see him again. The thought of seeing him filled me with anticipation and anxiety. My brain struggled to wrap itself around the intensity of our encounter and the implications it could have. Was this just a fleeting moment or something more significant? The good girl inside me knew I was treading dangerous waters, but my heart felt curious to dip its toe in.

As I lay there, unable to sleep, I noticed the wooden doors that enclosed the room, and my mind slipped back in time.

I am ten years old and I'm "in a mood," as Mom says. My

grandmother is over, and they're having tea in the living room. People are coming over soon and Mom's already asking me to get my songs ready. "Recital, recital!" she sings, pointing to the room she's dubbed "the piano room."

I hate playing for everyone. The way they all stare at me makes me nervous. I play piano for me, not for them, but she insists anyway. "I always wished I could play," she reminds me for the hundredth time, as if that should make me want to.

Mom can tell I'm cranky, so she urges me to "go get good Amber." I walk through the kitchen and into the garage, which smells like car exhaust and something else I don't like. I give myself the pep talk. *Don't be moody, be happy. Be good Amber, not bad Amber. Put on a smiling face and get back in there.*

I stand up straight, relax my shoulders, paint a smile on my face, and walk back through the doorway as if I've just stepped through a magical mood-altering portal. "Happy Amber is here!" I exclaim as I walk back into the living room. My mom and grandma cheer and clap their hands in applause. I laugh, and a part of me dies with it.

A very clear message forms in my mind:

Push your true feelings down; they're not welcome here.

Being a good girl is how you'll get love and praise.

Since meeting John, a similar tape has been playing in my head. *These feelings aren't real. This connection is just in your head. You're just sexually frustrated. And most important, you're very married. Be a good wife, not a bad wife.*

But a good wife can have soul friends, right?

The Messenger

A FEW WEEKS PRIOR TO MY KISMET MEETING with John, I called my intuitive—a modern-day medicine woman, if you will—for guidance. I check in with her once or twice per year when I feel stuck, and I had questions about my marriage, motherhood, the land project, and where my path was leading me. While I don't quite know how her process of "seeing into my future" and "connecting with my guides" works, I always walk away feeling more connected, clear, and at peace.

On this particular call, she tells me that a "messenger" is coming to the land project and it will alter the course of my life. You can imagine my surprise, then, when I discover that the name of my new soul friend is John *Messinger*, pronounced *messenger*, of course.

This is a detail I can't seem to get out of my mind two evenings later when John is sitting across from me at a dinner party—a long table of eight. My husband, wearing his investor and curator hat as per usual, made this dinner happen, wanting to introduce our new friends to other creatives in the area.

"It's time for you to get really honest with yourself," the

intuitive had repeated a few times before our call ended. "Do you hear me?"

"But I am honest with myself," I said, a little agitated. ". . . Am I not?"

She smiled but did not answer.

At dinner, John and I pick up right where we left off, like long-lost friends who haven't seen each other in years but are instantly in sync. He tells me one of the reasons he's in Todos Santos is because his mentor and meditation teacher encouraged him to come look at land here. And not only is he looking at land, he's curious to learn more about *our* project.

I decide at once this must mean only one thing: John is meant to be my design partner, *not* my life partner. Of course!

→-←

OUR PLANS TO DISCUSS the project at length coincide with a festival-themed birthday weekend my friend is throwing. Fifty of his closest friends are coming in to town to celebrate. This is the kind of party that is less like a birthday party and more like an intimate Burning Man meets sex soiree. Think: nearly nude costumes and psychedelic drugs. Live DJ sets and late-night dance moves. There's a bus parked on the property for sex play. For some, this is the kind of place that leads them to liberation. For me, it is my version of hell.

I witnessed too many wild parties in my parents' basement, including once walking in on the woman whose kids I babysat having sex with a man who wasn't her husband. As a child who grew up too fast, I had to be the one to turn down the music so I could get enough sleep. I hung NO SMOKING signs around the house to remind my mom and their friends to take their bad habit outside. Now, as an adult, wild parties still don't feel fun, but rather they make me feel uneasy—unsafe, even. Even though everything inside me yells "RUN!" when I find myself in this kind of environment, the birthday boy is a dear friend and I'm doing my damnedest to see this as an opportunity to push past my reservations and let go a little.

I invite John to join in on the festivities with a healthy warning—*Clothes are practically optional here,* I text him. *I think I can handle it,* he replies. John arrives just as dinner is ending and the party is starting. I catch his gaze from across the room, and my husband and I stand to walk toward him. "So good to see you, John," he says as he shakes his hand and pulls him in for a hug. "I want to thank you because I've never seen my wife more alive."

I've never seen my wife more alive.

That sentence etches itself into my heart like a carving on a tree trunk. *Alive.* Yes. That's it. That's what I'm feeling. *When did I stop feeling alive?*

"Oh, I don't know about that," John says, somewhat embarrassed. "I appreciate you saying so, and I'm genuinely moved to hear that you're feeling so alive, Amber."

Things *move* John. It's a quality about him that intrigues me. I notice the way he observes the light shifting in a space, the sound of palm trees rustling in the wind, and that moment when a frame comes into focus so he can capture it in his mind. He was a documentary photographer in his younger years and today he's an accomplished visual artist. It's clear to me that his creative mastery is directly linked to how he moves, and more so, how things move him.

My husband sees a few friends in the distance, says something charming, and walks away. "Can I get you something
to drink?" John asks, showing me the bottle of mezcal he
brought as a gift. What John doesn't know is that there's
no alcohol at this party. Let's just say it's not the drug of
choice. But being entirely sober as my heart hammers in my
throat, I'm relieved when he pours us one. We clink glasses,
and before we know it, a small group flocks around us to
meet the mysterious newcomer, and to sneak a drink of
their own. I introduce John to a few friends, and I notice
the women at this party seem to light up when they talk
to him. One of them tilts her head back, exposing her neck
as she laughs. Another places her hand on his arm, leaning in close to speak, her voice low and breathy. They play
with their hair, lick their lips, and stand a little too close,
their bodies angled toward him. John responds with kindness and respect, his polite smile unwavering. Yet I notice a
slight tension in his shoulders, a flicker of unease in his eyes
that mirrors my own.

I step away to find water and catch my breath—watching
John with other women is making me queasy. And the fact
that it's making me queasy makes me even *more* queasy. As
I navigate through the crowd, I bump into a woman named
Daniella. People have been telling me that I've needed to
meet her for years, and instantly I'm drawn to her energy
and spirit. She's bright and intuitive, and speaks expres-
sively with her entire body. We find a cozy corner to chat
and get to know each other.

Mid-conversation, she stops, grabs my arm, and points
across the yard. "That guy over there. Do you know that he's

your soulmate?" I stop breathing. I'm afraid to look. I turn my head, and she's pointing at John. Of course she's pointing at John. I start breathing again. She doesn't know John, nor has she ever met him. She also doesn't know that I know John or if I've ever met him. "There's this magnetic energy between you two," she says. "Almost like you're the same person, but different. Like two halves."

"Really?" I say casually. "That's crazy."

But nothing inside me feels casual about this.

Later that night John is talking to a friend of mine. A woman on my short list of "might be John's person." She's wearing a tight sparkly bodysuit that shows off her petite frame, and I wonder if he prefers a body like hers over a body like mine. She's laughing and touching his arm. *Wait, why is she touching his arm? Take your goddamn hand off him. Oh god, I think they're flirting. Is he flirting with her, too? I feel sick. I want to throw up. No, actually, I want to rip her head off.* This is not going well. This whole "introduce him to his person" thing. I need to move this energy through my body. I need to dance.

Tropical house music plays in the near distance, drawing me toward it. Thirty or so humans smile and sway under tall palm trees as neon lights shoot up into the sky. *Oh, there's my husband—I was wondering where he went.* I'm overwhelmed by the storm of jealousy brewing inside me, so I try to ignore it by dancing with my husband. Because that is what a good wife does. She dances with her *husband.* We dance for a few moments, smiling at each other, and then he turns to dance with everyone else, which is perfectly natural for us, and doesn't bother me one bit.

I turn with the breeze, and I notice John walk onto the

dance floor. He is alone. I hold my breath. He moves toward me. I'm not sure if I've resumed breathing. We slowly sway our bodies to the rhythm. He's a good dancer. We move naturally together, but we're also alone, in our own space, in our own movements. I want to know about his conversation with my friend, but I also want to play it cool.

"So what did you think of my friend?" I try and fail to say casually. "Might she be the kind of person you'd be into?"

He smiles. "I think a younger me would've been intrigued," he says, freeing me with relief. "But in all honesty, and please don't repeat this, she doesn't really feel entirely inside of herself. I think for me at this point in my life, I'm more interested in being with someone who cares less about what other people think."

"I understand that," I say. "Well, there seems to be plenty of interest in you at this party. The ladies love you, don't they?"

I blush, immediately embarrassed by what I said. *"The ladies love you, don't they?" What is going on with me?*

He laughs, brushing off my words. "I'm not only interested in that feeling of flames," he says. "I'm looking for something deeper than that. Maybe even safer than that."

"I get that," I say, relieved to learn more about what he finds attractive.

"For instance," he says, pausing briefly to consider his words. "And please know that I say this with the utmost respect, and I don't mean to overstep here at all, but if you had a sister, I would very much be interested in meeting her."

If I had a *sister*? My heart begins to race. My eyes widen and my cheeks flush. I giggle nervously and glance away.

Amber Rae

"I'm so sorry—I truly didn't mean that flirtatiously," he adds. "Is it okay that I said that?"

"Yes, of course," I say, glancing up at him. "I understand what you mean and I appreciate you saying it. Truly."

Our bodies relax and our eyes connect in unison. I let myself look a little longer, breathe a little deeper, and feel a little more. I don't look away or giggle nervously or quickly change the subject. I take him in, and I let him take me in. And in doing so, I let myself be seen.

Which hasn't happened in a while.

Maybe in Another Life

THE NEXT DAY, JOHN AND I ARE SITTING AT A CAFÉ in a palm grove, having breakfast and reviewing the architectural plans for the project. My husband and I have been working with an architect from Mexico City on the design. "Tell me honestly," I say. "What do you think?"

As he flips through the images, he squints and furrows his brow. I get the sense that he's the kind of man who has trouble hiding what he's thinking.

"You hate it, don't you?"

"Hate's a strong word," he says with a quick smile. "It's just . . . way too many arches," he explains, now more serious. "The house doesn't rest in the land. It sits on top of it. The natural environment gets lost, and everything is just too big. Honestly, it feels kind of colonial. Is it okay that I'm speaking so honestly?"

"Please," I say. "I'm designing this alone right now and need help. You can be transparent and direct with me. I hate reading between the lines."

"Oh good," he says, exhaling. "Me too."

John pulls out a pen and a small notepad that lives in his back pocket—the same one I use. He opens it to a blank page.

"So, when I think about everything that you've told me about this project, it seems to me that what moves you most about this whole thing is the land. The undeniable natural beauty of this place. So, I think the reason that you're not connecting with the plans so far is because of all the arches and pillars and grandeur—it's all just taking away from the part you love most. The land itself. I wonder if you've thought at all about minimalism as a design principle."

"Go on," I say, my curiosity piqued.

"Okay, well, forgive me if I'm saying anything that you know already. But the original minimalists were simply responding to the abstract expressionists. Let's use Jackson Pollock and his drip paintings as an example. He was saying that these drips and splatters of paint represent *me*, the artist, and everything that's going on inside *me*. And the minimalists were saying, that's great, Jackson, and it's beautiful too, but it's no longer just about *you*, the artist. That's not what matters most anymore. So they responded with blank canvases on the wall and bricks on the floor, because to the minimalists, art isn't just about the all-important maker, it's about the viewer, and how he or she perceives the world. So the blank canvas isn't just a blank canvas. It's a mirror. It's an invitation for the viewer to look at him or herself more closely, and to pay closer attention to how he or she perceives reality. Anyway, I'm sorry to ramble, but I think this place you're building is an opportunity to create a beautiful, natural mirror for people. A place for them to come, to be quiet and still, and to look at themselves with honesty and clarity . . ."

My whole body feels invigorated as John speaks. His words resonate on a level that I can't figure out how to put into words, except to say, "Mmmm, yes. That's it. That's it *exactly.*"

"So, for the design of this house, and for every turn on the land, I see each moment as an opportunity—a chance for you, the designer, to create a point of reflection, an invitation even—ultimately inviting the viewer to experience awe, beauty, and most important, a return to the Self."

He pauses here for a moment, as if he's coming up for air, or like he's a bit self-conscious after speaking so passionately—like he's let me see this new side of him and is hoping it's okay.

I smile encouragingly. "Please continue."

"When I think about this project, this piece of land, and what you want to achieve here, I keep coming back to two ideas: the mirror and the circle," he says. "The mirror as the point of reflection. *All that's left is you* kind of a thing. And the circle, as a symbol for wholeness and eternity. No more arches—arches are man-made and grandiose. Circles are natural, and honest, and whole."

"I don't know what to say," I muster, the air now filled with some unnamable charge. "You've been the missing piece for me this whole time."

John smiles and takes in my words. "Which reminds me . . . I've been thinking about what this project could be called, just as a working title of sorts, and the word that keeps coming to me is *espejo.*"

"Espejo," I repeat, letting the word sink in.

"It's 'mirror' in Spanish," he says.

"Yes, I love that word. *Espejo*," I say again. "It's beautiful."

"It's the place you come to see yourself more clearly," he says.

"How perfectly poetic," I say. "That's always been the goal of my writing and art."

"I know," he says as he looks into my eyes. "I remember you telling me. Mine too."

Time stops for a solid minute as we look at each other intently, like, *Hello, you. What's this that's happening here between us?*

I'm relieved when our moment of connection is interrupted by a squeal. Daniella, the apparent soulmate whisperer, is standing in front of our table with a few of her friends.

"You two!" she exclaims with her whole face. "You're here together! What kind of magic are you two cooking up?"

"We're in a design brainstorm about the land project I'm working on. John is blowing my mind over here."

Daniella squeezes her hands together in delight. "That's wonderful," she says. "So very wonderful. May we do a planting ceremony?"

"A what . . . ?"

"May we bless the magic that is occurring between the two of you here?"

John and I look at each other and laugh. I sense that he finds this offer as odd and delightful as I do.

"Oh, please do," I say, smiling.

Daniella and her friends begin to walk around our table in a circle. "We're planting seeds, planting seeds, planting seeds!" she says in a singsongy way as she flutters her fingers down like rain falling. "And watering them, watering them, watering them! And culllltivating, culllltivating, culllltivating . . . so beautiful things can grow, can grow, can grow!"

Loveable

The dance around our table stops and we all have a laugh. She winks at me as she walks away.

"So where were we?" I ask. "Circles and mirrors?"

"Circles and mirrors."

We leave breakfast and head to a design and furniture gallery down the road to get a sense of the design details we both like. On the drive, John tells me about his long and winding relationship with birds.

"I know it sounds strange but eight different birds have killed themselves on my car," he says, pausing to let his words land. I gasp. That's *not* what I was expecting. "The first time it happened, I was eighteen—an owl just swooped right into my driver's side window. It then proceeded to happen every few years or so with a new bird. I went to see my meditation teacher, Peter, and he asked me out of nowhere, 'Do you know about the birds?' And I said, 'Yes, Peter, I know about the birds! What's up with the birds?' He told me that the birds are trying to wake me up and tell me that I'm a bird too. That I can fly. I don't need to tuck in my wings out of fear of what might happen to me if I'm my full, authentic self. He said the bird is the connection between the heavens and the earth, and they're ultimately a wake-up call for me, reminding me to fly."

We park in front of the design and furniture gallery and walk inside. We look around the space, pointing to decor, furniture, lamps, and lighting fixtures we like. I take a seat in a chair to test its comfort, and John sits in another across from me. "This is cushy," I say, crossing my legs and leaning forward. When I look up, John's eyes find mine, and we hold each other's gaze for a little longer than usual. The intensity of the moment leaves me breathless, a silent question hanging in the air between us.

"There's something weighing on me that I want to bring up, but I'm not really sure how," I say, pausing briefly to consider my words, my pulse rising.

John looks at me, a hint of concern on his brow. "Please," he says. "I'd love to hear."

"Okay, I'm not very good at leaving things unsaid, so I'll just say this outright: I'm noticing that I feel a strong connection between us, and it's taken me by surprise. So I guess I'm just trying to make sense of it. Is it just me, or are you feeling this too?"

"Yes, of course," he says, shifting in his seat and sitting taller. "I really do appreciate you speaking honestly and bringing this up. I'd be lying if I said I hadn't noticed it too."

"So what do you think this is?" I ask.

"Well . . ." He pauses, looking up and then looking back at me. "In all candor, the night we met, I had this feeling of recognition at first sight with you—like time collapsed and I instantly knew you, and had for some time. It's something I've never quite experienced before."

"That was also my experience," I say, relieved. "Almost like we've been together in . . . um . . ."

"Another life?"

"Yeah, exactly," I say with a nervous laugh.

"So, at first I was sad about it, and a little frustrated, if I'm being honest, like why is the universe introducing me to a person who is clearly a soulmate but who's not available to me and is in what appears to be a happy marriage?" he says.

I nod as fireworks go off inside me. Something about the way he says "appears to be" makes me listen closer.

"But what I've come to realize is that I think we've been brought together to show each other what love can feel like when we don't need to possess each other. We can see each other fully and root for each other without needing to be together. Your presence is showing me what's possible—what the most honest, real, and unconditional kind of love can feel like."

"We're mirrors," I say. "Espejo."

"Exactly," he says. "Espejo."

I notice John's gaze move quickly to the door, and then slide across the room, settling slightly above my head. His mouth opens and his eyes widen. I follow his eyes, turning my body around to see what he's looking at. Above my head is a large round mirror mounted to the wall that two small finches have landed on. One has red, black, and white feathers. The other has muted brown. They are both chirping as if in conversation. They look at themselves in the mirror, and then they look at each other, and then they look at us. This goes on for a few minutes. And as suddenly as they arrived, they fly away.

⇒ ⇐

LATER, WHEN I RECOUNT this story to a friend and how wild it all seemed, she stops me and says point-blank, "You're so used to love being hard that you never learned it could be easy. This is what ease feels like."

Ease. Wouldn't that be nice.

What I Learned About Love

WHEN MY MOM WAS PREGNANT WITH ME, MY DAD fucked her best friend. He then barely made it on time to my birth because he was "busy." Two years later he traveled across the country to follow his dream of becoming a musician, and started a new life with a new woman. He did not pay child support, nor did he tell my mom where exactly he had relocated. She found out later when she heard about his car accident on the news. "He was the great love of my life," my mom would say, her words followed by a cloud of smoke from her Newport menthol. "But we were too young and dumb."

He was the great love of my life.

That line always stood out to me like a statement in therapy begging to be unpacked. Does the great love of your life leave me and you—and then *vanish*? Is feeling intense and overwhelming feelings for someone who is not available or present *great love*—or is that *great wounding*?

But then I'd look at my mom, in her blue jeans, black shirt, and stilettos, leaning back in her chair, legs crossed on top of her desk, looking all boss-like and in control, and I'd wonder: *Would my father and her love each other now if they could start over? Would he love me, too?*

My mom is what I'd call a hippie powerhouse. She grew up in the 1970s and is all about peace and love, but she's also one of the most resilient, don't-fuck-with-me people I've ever known. If it were possible for a flower child and a mobster to merge—but without all the bad intent and dead people—that would be my mom. She's tough. She's fierce. So tough and fierce that she chose to build a business in the male-dominated field of construction, with teams of men working for her. She'd take me to her job sites when I was a teen—her in stilettos with spikes, me in wedges—just to prove to me that women can do anything they put their minds to, in exactly the way they like. When a man doubted her abilities, proving him wrong was her favorite challenge of all.

Mom believed that if you think it and believe it, it will happen, which she reminded me and our extended family when she handed out copies of *The Law of Attraction*. I was hooked. Her confidence in the power of mindset was contagious, and I'd find myself visualizing my future and believing there was no impossible goal. But as important as belief was, she taught me that the real magic was in the action that followed. Mom never waited for things to fall in her lap. She went out and grabbed them with both hands.

Her approach to life was unconventional, and so was her parenting. She was the one to introduce me to pot in high school (because, you know, it was safer that way), but she was also the bouncer at my birthday party, turning away anyone who looked like they were "up to no good." Mom could smell bullshit a mile away—except when it came to love.

When I was nine, my mom married a man our whole family loved. It all seemed good and well at first. He was charismatic and clean-cut, he loved my mom and was kind to me, and she appeared happy. I had high hopes. On the day of their wedding, after much thought and consideration, I told him with all the sincerity of a nine-year-old, "I'm going to call you Dad now." If I couldn't have my father, maybe this replacement dad would do. I mean, what could possibly go wrong?

As it turns out, a lot. By the time I was sixteen, my mom was often distraught over his unwelcome involvement in her business and finances. He once cornered me in his office, screaming, to try to convince me that she was cheating on him with her best friend and business partner, who also happened to be gay. Because my stepdad was the kind of man I once found drunk, on a beach, hitting on college girls, and because he would make comments to me like "The space between your legs looks nice" and "When you get hair on your nipples, you should shave them," it was not difficult for me to call bullshit. But because he was also a former college football player and twice my size, I stood there frozen like a deer in headlights as his spit from screaming landed on my face.

This incident happened to be the last straw for my mom— thank god—and for the next twenty years, this man would continue to write me letters every few years about how *I* had abandoned *him*, and how his only regret with me was that he had smoked. But I was still his daughter, he'd write, and he loved and missed me very much. Even today, after all these years, his words haunt me. I haven't spoken to him since I was twenty, yet I still argue with him in my mind.

This pattern of choosing unreliable and unavailable men didn't start and stop with my mom. My mom's father left my grandma for his secretary. My dad's father left my grandma for her best friend. Many of the women in my family line have their own version of the men they loved and how they were betrayed by them. Somewhere along the way, a very clear message formed in my mind:

Do not trust men you are in love with. Instead, choose relationships where you hold the power and control. This is how you stay safe.

The Surrender Experiment

"HOW DOES YOUR HUSBAND FEEL ABOUT ALL THIS?" My friend Erin's question about my growing connection with John made me pause. I'm ashamed to admit that, in all my excitement about John, I hadn't really stopped to consider how my husband might be feeling. He seemed fine—he hadn't said anything, which I took to mean that he was okay with everything. But a deeper part of me knew he was likely having feelings about all this.

The last thing I wanted to do was hurt my husband, but I also couldn't ignore the pull to make sense of my bond with John. While the good-girl part of me cares very much about my husband's feelings, I also notice a resentful part of me coming online that wants to give fewer fucks. A likely side effect of feeling like my needs hadn't been considered for years, a rebelliousness and righteousness has taken hold: I deserve to feel this—even if it makes my husband uncomfortable. *This is good for him*, I'd convinced myself.

And in some ways, it actually was. Shortly after meeting

John, my husband told me, "I've been a sleeping bear and now John has woken me up. His presence is confronting, but it's also a gift." In a matter of weeks, I witnessed my husband evolve from a possessed workaholic to a man more present and in tune. He was listening to the book *The Surrender Experiment* when John arrived, and I watched as he attempted to put the key principle into practice: to let go of control and embrace life's flow.

When I told my husband I wanted John involved in the project because he was my ideal design collaborator, he was instantly onboard. It wasn't a hard sell—he also saw that John's magnetism, confidence, and expertise would be a big draw for investors and collaborators. I was pleasantly surprised, however, when an unusual alliance formed: he and John were developing their own relationship. John helped him set up a meditation altar, talked to him about consistent self-care practices, and offered brotherly wisdom. They'd smoke a spliff together on the roof and wax poetic on life. It moved me.

When the three of us were together, the chemistry was palpable. Resources and opportunities seemed to come out of nowhere to help make the land project possible. While the three of us acknowledged that something unusual and hard to explain was brewing between us, we kept coming back to the same intention: surrender and trust. This seemed to open doors for all three of us. . . .

"I feel like I found my John," my husband said one day when we were out boating with a group of friends. While I was on the ground level, chatting with Erin, he was on the top, having an experience with another woman. "I was gazing into her eyes, with my hand on her thigh, lost in the moment with her—totally transfixed. When it dawned on me that you might walk upstairs and see me, I panicked. But I also found myself thinking that maybe this is okay too . . ."

Hearing him share this did not upset me. I felt excited for him. Relieved, even. I *wanted* him to experience that kind of connection. Hell, I wanted him to put his hand on another woman's inner thigh more than I wanted him to put his hand on mine. And what I realized most of all was that I wanted John to touch me. I hadn't yet let my mind go there. Thinking about us being physical felt like crossing a line. But why? Because I made a vow? I wondered at what point vows stop being promises that support our growth and start becoming invisible chains, trapping us in patterns we've never questioned, afraid that if we reach for what we truly want, we might lose it all.

A few days later, in the midst of land-project planning, my husband sat both John and me down. He said, "Ever since John came onto the project, it's created so much space for me. I've always wanted to be famous and make a big impact, and with you two spending so much time together, I now feel like I have the time to do just that."

I've always wanted to be famous.

That sentence gave me pause. I'd always known he wanted to do important work in the world, but fame? He hadn't mentioned that in the nine years I'd known him. But when he said it, I knew it to be true. His relentless work ethic, his enormous visions "to change the world," his constant networking—he wanted to do good, sure, but he also wanted to be *known*. It made me question his motivations and wonder how much his need for affirmation was running the project and show. While I understand the hunger for success and the desire to be seen—it's a feeling I know all too well—I'm also learning that it can come from a place of wounding, not wholeness. Looking for validation from others never seems to fill that inner void; it only leaves me searching for more, more, *more*.

His admission made me wonder if he, too, was chasing significance as a way to quiet something deeper—a longing, a fear, or an emptiness he hadn't yet named. I wondered, too, if this had been a shadow over our relationship all along, or perhaps a driving current. I'd always felt like a distant priority behind the next goal, the next big thing. He always denied this, of course. "You and our relationship are my number-one priority," he'd say. But I never believed him. And now, in this moment, I understand why.

The Dangerous Truth

SO MUCH HAPPENS OVER THE NEXT FEW DAYS that time starts to bend—days feel like months, with each moment packed so full it's hard to keep up. Everything carries a weight, a significance, like the universe is dialing up the intensity and asking me to pay attention.

When the three of us are out to dinner with a potential investor one night, he starts telling us about an artwork in his collection that is meditative and deeply important to him. "A tapestry of Polaroids," he describes it, and I notice John sit a little taller in his seat. When he pulls out his phone to show us a photo, it turns out to be one of John's commissioned works. The coincidence feels uncanny, as if something larger is quietly steering us along.

The next afternoon, famous chefs from around Mexico are in town for a series of events centered on food and drink, and the three of us decide to go. All day, people keep addressing John and me as if we're the married couple. "Oh no, he's not my husband," I correct them with a polite smile, gesturing to my husband. "He is." Their responses are always the same—an awkward "Oh," followed by a quick change of subject. John and I exchange a look, amused and a little uneasy.

Later that day, we stop by a new boutique hotel for a drink. My husband opens up about how he feels like he's coming more into himself, thanking John for being a catalyst in this shift. I still don't fully understand what the hell is happening here, but I keep trying to trust and let go of needing to know. As we're leaving, I grab both their hands and say, "The story's already written; we're just learning the lines." It feels like the truest thing I've said in weeks, free from trying to figure out what happens next.

It's in this charged, surreal whirlwind of days that I find myself sipping mezcal on the porch with John, just the two of us. Waves crash in the background as Andrew Bird plays in the foreground. Once again my husband has gone to bed early, and while I should be tired—I've barely slept for a week—I've never felt more alive.

John's been staying with us for the last few nights while we work on the project. These late-night chats have become our thing—the moments when we talk about art and life and everything in between. We've been asking each other questions all night, enveloped in a cocoon of vulnerability and safety and wanting to know every last thing about the other. It's John's turn to ask me a question.

"What's the name of the band your father played in?" he asks. "I hope you don't mind, but I've been doing a little bit of research, and I may have found a woman in Nashville from his era who could help you track down his music."

If there are words for this moment, I can't find them. I just sit there, looking at him, stunned. A few nights ago, briefly and in passing, I mentioned that I'd never heard my father's singing voice. He died in that same hospital where I'd visited him when I was eight, and while I was told there was a box of his recordings, it was never found. John didn't say anything, but by the way his brow furrowed and his eyes narrowed, he said everything.

"The band was called Dreamer," I say. "But when he moved to Nashville, he started playing solo under his first and middle name, Michael Paul."

"Your father's middle name was Paul?" John asks as he leans toward me.

"Yes . . ."

"Paul was my father's middle name too. Martin Paul."

"Of course it was," I say, smiling. "Michael and Martin Paul. You know . . . since my dad's death, I've felt his presence in my life, almost like he's able to support me more as a spirit than he ever would have been able to as a father. And I know this is heavy and perhaps a bit far-fetched, but I've been having this feeling that somehow our fathers are responsible for bringing us together. Like they've had a hand in all of this." As the words leave my mouth, a shooting star falls from the sky and into the sea, adding an exclamation point to my words.

"Did you see that?" I asked.

"No," he said. "But I saw you see it, which was even better."

I look at him, his eyes fixed on me. There's that blooming feeling again. "I may not be able to tell you this again," he says, looking at his hands and then up at me. "And I'm not sure I should be saying it at all, but . . ." He says this next part slowly, syllable by syllable, almost at a whisper. "I am so in love with you."

"What did you say?" I ask, the air leaving my body.

He looks me deep in the eyes, and says, "You heard me."

I want to say, *I'm so in love with you too. I've never wanted anyone to say those words more. They've never felt more right, more honest, more true. Let's leave together now, and let everything else burn to the ground.*

But instead I'm suddenly overwhelmed by my fear, my past, the potential consequences, what other people will think, and the reality of my situation. And so I say, also in a whisper, with anguish on my face, "Please don't say that again."

⇀–↽

I QUIETLY OPEN THE door of my bedroom and slowly tiptoe inside. When I lock the door behind me, I hear my husband stir. We're back to sleeping in the same room now that John is staying in our guest room. He's sitting up in bed, awake, arms crossed. I walk closer, but he won't look at me. When I try to touch him, he pulls away. I sit on my side of the bed, heart racing, as I watch beads of sweat drip down his forehead.

"Are you falling in love with him?" he asks pointedly.

I pause and consider my words carefully. I'm still trying to wrap my head and heart around what is happening, let alone what I'm actually feeling, but I also don't want to keep him in the dark. I want to be fair. I want to be true. I've been avoiding my truth for years, and this is a chance to practice radical honesty, even if the thought of doing so makes me nauseous.

"I think so," I say as softly as words can be said and still be heard. "I'm so sorry. I didn't see this coming at all, and I still don't know what it all means, but . . ." I stop, realizing the truth of the words before I say them aloud. "I've never felt this way before."

He exhales deeply and turns away from me. "I'm happy for you, I really am. I'm glad you're experiencing this. But if the roles were reversed, you would not be okay with this. Just because you have sexual chemistry with someone doesn't mean you can build a life with them."

Maybe he's right. Maybe this is crazy. Maybe I'm just turned on. Good wives don't hurt their husbands, even if that means they're hurting themselves. They compromise, bury their desires, and push their own needs aside to keep the peace. They figure it out. They make it work. They keep trying. Even if they've been trying for so long.

I'm Fine

WHEN JOHN FIRST TOLD ME HE WAS IN LOVE WITH me and I said, "Please don't say that again," my initial instinct was to pull away. I was afraid, the stakes felt too high, and I couldn't bear the thought of hurting my husband. So, over the next few days, I began building walls between me and John. In the midst of this, John asked me to go for coffee. We sat on a concrete bench and looked out at a grove of lush palm trees.

After a long silence, he says, "I'm sorry if what I said put you in an uncomfortable position. I would blame the mezcal, but obviously, there's something here. I've noticed you pulling away, and this has also given me time to think. I think you're extraordinary, and clearly there is a soulmate connection between us, but I think we need to put to bed whatever it is that's arising here. If we're going to do this project and be design partners, we have to let this part of our connection die. I don't mean this as an ultimatum and you haven't done anything wrong, truly, but I can't continue to long for someone I can't have. It just brings up too much old wounding for me, and I need to protect my little boy."

He says this while tapping his finger on the center of his

chest, a slight tremble in his voice. I want to reach my hand to his—to reassure him, to let him know our connection is safe, but instead, I grip the bench to steady myself.

"I've learned too many times before with unavailable partners," he continues, "that if I stay in this in-between place with you, it won't work for either of us. I'll start to become inauthentic, I'll start angling for an outcome, and I'll begin to resent this situation. I need to be open to the kind of love that's available to me, and the reality is, you're simply not available."

"I understand," I say, glancing down, feeling suddenly ill.

"We need to shift the care and love we feel for each other into a genuine friendship dynamic. You're going to have to be okay with me meeting my person and having a family— just like I'm going to have to be okay with that for you. We can't be secretly in love with each other for the duration of the life that we're about to spend together."

"Okay . . ." I say, looking at John, nose tingling, eyes welling with tears. He looks at me, closes his eyes for a few moments, exhales deeply, and then places his hand on top of mine.

"Listen," he says softly, eyes moist. "This hurts me too. But sometimes the timing just doesn't align and sometimes the story doesn't turn out the way we want it to."

"I understand," I say again, now weeping. "It's okay, really. I'm fine."

I'm fine.

Even when my heart is breaking, tears are dripping down my face, and I'm very much *not* fine, my instinct is to say "I'm fine"—two words that have haunted me throughout my life.

My mom and stepdad's behavior is making me feel unsafe?

I'm fine. I can be the strong and wise one.

I feel mistreated in this friendship?

I'm fine. I probably deserve it.

I'm feeling serious doubts about getting married?

I'm fine. I'll figure it out.

My husband and I aren't having sex?

I'm fine. Maybe I can do without.

People will be mad at me if I leave my marriage?

I'm fine. I can stay and work this out.

The man whose love I'm too afraid to embrace tells me that he needs to move on?

I'm fine. We can just be friends.

I became masterful at saying, "I'm fine" because no one had been there when I *wasn't* fine. Growing up, the adults didn't know how to appropriately support me when I said, "I'm not okay. I'm hurting. This is hard. I'm not fine." And when I did share my honest feelings, the adults tended to either brush them off or get so overwhelmed by how my feelings made them feel that I was left to manage their reactions rather than get the support I needed.

So "I'm fine" became the Thing that gave me peace of mind. The Thing that helped me forge ahead. The Thing that shielded me from pain and vulnerability.

And yet, it was also the Thing that kept me small.

After John spoke his truth and I told him "I'm fine," he stunned me when he broke the long silence and said, "Well, I'm not fine. I'm actually really fucking sad."

I was taken aback. In awe. Moved by his emotional honesty. It had never occurred to me until that moment that I could say, "I'm not fine." How freeing.

Because beneath "I'm fine," my truth was this: *Fuck, I'm*

going to lose John, this man who I'm pretty sure might be my person. I'm going to see him fall in love with another woman. What the hell am I doing? I'm very much not fine. I'm really fucking sad too. This life I've created isn't working. What am I doing?

In this moment, an essential realization took hold of me: I realized I was choosing to sit back in a friendship masquerading as a marriage while I would one day watch my soulmate who I was pretending was my friend fall in love with another person. Suddenly, the thought of losing John and betraying my true desires felt far more painful than leaving my marriage and hurting my friend. Both options were going to hurt, but what I started to consider was which one would hurt me *more*. I realized that I could keep pretending that I was fine, it was workable, everything could be figured out, and no one had to get hurt. Or I could simply acknowledge that I wasn't fine, hadn't been, and this could no longer continue. By finally admitting "I'm not fine," I was breaking the cycle of silence and self-denial. I was creating the space for what was most true.

The Talk

I FIND MY HUSBAND PACING AROUND THE HOUSE in a fury, looking for his keys. "Where's John? I'm going to find him," he says, and then drives off in a hurry, leaving a cloud of dust in his wake.

I text John to give him a heads-up. He's at a café, writing. My husband, it turns out, has already reached out to him because "they need to talk." Feeling in the dark and out of the loop unsettles me.

Later I'll learn that my husband came in hot, saying, "You're trying to steal my wife! Are you in love with her?"

"I am," John said. "I never expected any of this to happen. And I really adore you. I truly mean that."

"But that's *my* wife," my husband kept repeating.

"I know she is," John said. "And can I ask you an honest question?"

My husband nodded.

"Please don't take this the wrong way, but you keep repeating she's your wife, so why aren't you acting like it?"

Suddenly he softened. He put the armor down. He shuffled in his seat and paused for a brief moment.

"I don't know," he said eventually. They ended up speaking

for over an hour as two friends, both going through some- thing they'd never experienced before. My husband went on to admit to John that he didn't know what he wanted anymore but that he'd sacrificed so much for me and the re- lationship. He told him that he knew he wanted to be suc- cessful in work, but he didn't know how to show up for the relationship anymore.

"There's no road map for this," John said, now sus- pecting that I wasn't the only one who wanted out of this relationship—a commitment that had gone on for too long because two people were afraid to look at the truth, let alone speak it.

→-←

THE NEXT EVENING, THE three of us set foot down a dirt road toward the sea. When we reached the beach, I was so awestruck by the beauty that I invited them to lay down in the sand with me and look up at the blanket of stars above. We stayed there for a long while in silence, feeling the salt on our skin, the crashing Pacific below, the vast ink above.

"It's time for me to call it a night, but you two stay," my husband said as he stood up, breaking the silence. My breath caught in my chest, and my body tightened.

"Are you sure?" John asked, moving to stand with him.

"Why would I get in the way of the magic that is the two of you?" he said. "It's undeniable."

My body relaxed.

"Are you sure you don't want to stay?" I asked, in some way hoping he wouldn't.

"No, no—you stay," he said, walking away. "Enjoy."

John and I looked at each other, opening and closing our

mouths, searching for words we couldn't seem to find. We lay there for what felt like a lifetime. The silence between us was easy and familiar. He extended his left arm and I scootched over to him, our sides pressed up against each other for the first time. Electricity. I laid my head on his shoulder, our pulses quickening.

"You know how I said that I was going to match you with your person?" I said, breaking the silence.

"Yes."

"I don't want to do that anymore."

"Why?"

"I think I want to keep you as my person."

John inhaled and then exhaled slowly, and then said, "That's the nicest thing you've ever said to me."

As much as my heart was fully in this moment with John, my mind was also on that walk back home with my husband. While I can't pretend to know what he was thinking when he left John and me on the sand dune, I can imagine that leaving your wife with another man—a man perhaps more suited to her, a man she has undeniable chemistry with, a man who's ready and available to meet her in ways you haven't been able to—would feel heartbreaking, even if it was also relieving.

Though I wondered if this was an opening for him, too. Earlier in the day, he had broken down with me, sharing how he felt he had been abandoning himself and his priorities. Maybe this offered a chance for him to return to himself as well. Still, I found myself feeling anguish and aliveness at once—torn between the pain of hurting my friend and the longing to experience this kind of connection with John.

Overwhelmed by the unknown, I remind myself to keep practicing the surrender and trust that had gotten us this far. But my god was it uncomfortable—like standing on the shore of something vast, something unknown, unsure if I'd sink or soar.

Hand-Carved Wooden Doors

I'M LYING IN BED, SHEETS WRAPPING ME IN A cocoon, my cat Leo stretched out against my right thigh. My journal is open on my lap, urging me to be honest, begging me to name what's most true. I'm scared that my feelings for John are crazy, that I can't possibly fall in love this quickly, that good wives don't fall in love with other people. But I'm tired of trying to convince myself.

At the top of a fresh page, I write the question I always ask when I lead journaling workshops:

What truth are you afraid to admit to yourself, and why?

I take a deep breath and write, *I think I'm falling in love with John*, the words barely legible from my shaking hand. I let the sentence sit there and stare back at me for a while. Something about it doesn't feel fully honest, and then it dawns on me. I cross out *I think* and then *falling*, so all that's left is *I'm in love with John*. My pen continues without hesitation: *But there are so many reasons I should NOT be in love with John*—strong emphasis on the *NOT*.

I tap my pen, considering this.

For starters, I'm married. This fact alone has left me feeling ashamed and deeply confused and like a terrible person.

Second, I've only known John for a few weeks. Can I really be in love with him? And even if I am, am I really about to blow up my life for someone I just met?

Third, not only did we just close on a plot of land to build our family home, it was thanks, in part, to the financial support of my husband's mother and sister. I'm close with his family. This would devastate them. They are kind and warm and generous people whom I adore. I can't do this to them.

Fourth, I've made this all so much more complex by making John my design partner on the land project.

What on earth have I gotten myself into?

My phone buzzes, bringing me back into the room. It's a text from Erin, who always has impeccable timing. She has a vague idea of what's going on and she's been checking in on me every few days since, but I have yet to give her a full update on how I'm feeling.

How are you, my beauty? her text says.

I'm . . . good?

Good? That sounds unsure :)

A lot is happening. Feeling a lot. Really overwhelmed.

She FaceTimes immediately.

"Talk to me," she says in her usual warm, matter-of-fact way. Her beautiful, familiar face glows on the screen—enough to make me cry.

I spill my guts in full for the first time. I tell her that John feels like the person I want to build a life with, and how every second with him feels right. I tell her that I never knew that love and connection could feel this way.

I tell her that I love my husband, but I'm not in love with him. I tell her how terrified I am of hurting him, how disappointed people will be with me, how much I will be shamed and misunderstood, how crazy and impossible this all seems. Speaking candidly like this feels both freeing and frightening, as if speaking the words aloud means I can no longer hide from them.

I expect her to tell me that this is crazy and impossible. That I should stay in my marriage. That acting on my truth is too dangerous, too risky, and will cause too much pain. I expect the question: *How well do you really know this guy?* I'm prepared to defend myself. I'm prepared to feel ashamed. But she is not surprised, and she does not think this is a bad idea. In fact, she's smiling and nodding in a reassuring way. There's a brightness in her eyes. She doesn't look scared or afraid. She looks solid and at peace.

"It sounds like you're getting really clear about where you haven't been satisfied and how the story of your marriage doesn't match up with the reality of it," she says. "John's presence is a beautiful reflection and gift. How wonderful."

Her words settle me. "But isn't this selfish? Wrong?"

"Choosing what you really want and desire is not selfish," she says. "Your husband won't benefit from being in a relationship where you're not satisfied. No one wins. Liberation is a two-way street."

"But what if things don't work out with John? I've only known him for a few weeks."

"Maybe John is a catalyst; maybe he's the love of your life. Your job isn't to know where this all goes. Do one thing at a time, and you'll see. You don't need to have all the answers just yet."

"But the project. Our investors. Our friends. Our families. So many people are going to be disappointed in me."

"Sure, none of this is going to be easy, but when you make the courageous choice, it will align each person to the right thing. Some people will have feelings about this, but that's their stuff, not yours."

"What do I do?"

She smiles and pauses in a way that says, *You know what to do.* I pull the covers over my face and make an *ughhh* noise. "Okay, okay," I call up to the ceiling. "I know what to do."

"Of course you do," she says. "Don't delay the inevitable."

Don't delay the inevitable.

I let those words linger like a bell ringing, clear and undeniable, daring me to step fully into the unknown.

We hang up and I exhale deeply for what feels like the first time in weeks. I look across the room at the antique hand-carved wooden doors that enclose the room. The details look more vivid now. The intricacies of the carvings and the intentionality that went into each engraving mirror the care I want to put into designing my own life. It feels like the doorway is beckoning me to make a choice. . . .

I can give myself a pep talk: *Be a good wife, not a bad wife. Let your feelings for John go; they're too unknown. You can figure this out with your husband; keep putting in the work. Put on a smiling face and get back in there.*

Or I can give myself an honest talk: *You are a thirty-five-year-old woman and you get to decide how your life goes. You do not need to make choices to satisfy the needs and desires of other people. Sometimes you have to disappoint others so as not to disappoint yourself. Stop letting other people be the excuse for your not being brave. This is your life—grab hold.*

The doorway is no longer a mood-altering portal into a life of pleasing and performance; it's now a passageway into a life I intentionally create.

It's time to leave my marriage. It's time to give John and me a shot. Most of all, it's time to choose myself.

Transitions

TWO DAYS LATER MY HUSBAND AND I ARE SITTING on two stools, face-to-face, cheeks wet with tears, trying to have "the talk." How on earth are two people who've spent nearly a decade together supposed to say goodbye?

I rented a peaceful Airbnb so I could get some time alone to think. But alas, here we are. My husband stands, walks around the room, and pauses in front of an art piece on the wall. It says, *An invisible thread connects those who are destined to meet, regardless of time, place, or circumstance. The thread may stretch or tangle, but it will never break.*

Our paths were meant to cross, I know this with all of me. It felt destined the day I met him, twenty-six years young. He caught my attention from across the room with his warmth, heart, and gregarious spirit. But just because two people are fated to meet doesn't mean they're destined to stay together forever. Sometimes growth means growing apart.

My husband finally settles his pacing and sits back on the stool across from me.

"It's time to transition our marriage into a friendship," he says before I have the chance to, catching me by surprise. He'll admit later that he knew our marriage was over the night John and I met. He felt it too. I tell him that I'm deeply sorry for hurting him. He tells me that it's not my job to emotionally caretake him anymore; it's time for him to be a father to himself.

I tell him that I hold his true happiness in my heart, and it's also time for me to honor my own. Even though this is hard and painful, I believe in the deepest part of me that this is what's right and true for both of us—even if that's difficult to see right now. We hug, we cry, and we agree to move through our separation with as much love and care as we can muster.

He stands, grabs his bag, and looks back at me one last time before he walks out the front door. I expect grief to overwhelm me in this moment, but instead I'm met with relief.

I realize later that the gnawing ache that had been growing in me slowly and steadily over the years—*that* was grief. The hundreds of micro-moments of saying, "It's fine" when it was really "not fine." The constant pleading for emotional connection, for meaningful time together. Telling him again and again that I needed his actions and words to line up so I could feel safe—only to be disappointed, time and time again, when they didn't.

The truth is, I have already processed this loss—the anger, the sadness, the disappointment, the hope, the despair. I grieved our marriage while I was in it. And now that I've spoken my truth, I feel free. And at peace.

After a quiet morning with myself to process my new reality, I call John. Without saying hello, I say for the first time, "I'm so in love with you."

He receives my words with an audible breath and then

silence. In that moment, I realize the depths of how well I know him—knowing that he's taking his time, choosing his words thoughtfully, with that big open heart of his, swallowing back tears.

"You just made me the happiest man alive," he says, his voice breaking.

And for the first time in a long time, I feel like the happiest woman too.

Reborn

BARELY AN HOUR LATER JOHN IS PICKING ME UP to visit the local botanical gardens. The original plan was for John, my husband, and I to all go together to get design inspiration for the land project, but that plan has obviously changed.

I don't know what you're supposed to wear on what feels like your first official date with your soulmate, right after you have the divorce conversation with your soon-to-be ex-husband, but I decide on a short red linen dress with ruffled shoulders. I feel like I should have more feelings about how quickly things are moving, but the truth is, nothing about this feels fast—it only feels right.

I hear John's music playing and when I peer out the window, I see him parked. I walk outside and he steps out of the car, his eyes following my every step. This quality about him—his presence, the way he takes me in—still makes me nervous, but I also like it very much. I get into his car, put my seat belt on, and slip my hand into his. Sparks. I try to be a helpful copilot along the way by assisting with navigation and directions, but John turns to me and gently says, "You know, you don't have to drive all the time." I feel my entire body breathe a sigh of relief.

We arrive at the gardens, a sprawling campus that invites you to wander from garden to garden, country by country—from the Australian desert to the English rose gardens to the Japanese Zen garden—it's unlike anything I've ever seen. We walk through a psychedelic maze of succulents and out through a bamboo grove until we arrive at a bench in front of a lily pond. We sit, weeping willows dripping down around us. I don't know how we get there, but the next thing I know, we're comparing baby names we like, which makes every cell in my body smile. I'm keenly aware that from the outside in, talking about baby names this quickly might sound unhinged, but nothing about it feels rushed.

It seems like other people can sense how special this day is to us too. As we walk through the rose gardens, an older woman named Kate who reminds me of my grandmother, also named Kate, stops us to comment on how special our energy is together. "You remind me of my late husband and me," she says. "He passed just a few years back. He was the love of my life."

When we round the corner, we step foot into a field of Venetian sculptures that take my breath away. We find an older gentleman sitting on an Italian fountain, smiling at us. An artist, I gather, with his beret, paint-splattered pants, and look of hard-earned wisdom in his eyes. "Can I take your photograph?" he asks. "Two cosmic lovers." John and I look at each other and smile, touched by how others are reflecting us back to us. "I usually prefer to be behind the camera,"

John says, with his surprising but endearing modesty. "But yes—I'd love for you to capture this moment, thank you."

The gardens are starting to close, so we walk back to our car, hand in hand. We drive through the mountains, wind blowing through our hair, to a restaurant and wine room that looks like an old Western film set. Each outdoor table has a landscape painting hung above it, and peacocks roam the property. We stay long past dark, sipping pinot noir, talking nonstop. The feelings of excitement and deep peace course through me simultaneously, and I realize that this is the best day of my life.

At night's end, John holds me. Nothing more. We lie in bed like ancient lovers, as if it's the millionth time. His warm breath on the back of my neck sends shivers down my spine as I frame this moment in my mind, praying it never ends.

The next morning, I text a girlfriend the photo the stranger took of John and me in the garden. "You look reborn," she writes.

"I *feel* reborn," I reply.

⇒·⇐·

SOON JOHN WILL BE traveling abroad for six weeks, a work commitment he agreed to long ago. *Six* weeks! I've only known him for that long and it feels like a lifetime already. The thought of not seeing him for so long makes me queasy, but John settles me. "We'll FaceTime every day."

I call my mom to fill her in on what's been going on. "Don't freak out," I say.

"What?" she says back.

Amber Rae

"I don't know how else to say this, but . . . I'm leaving my marriage."

"Because of that other guy?" she asks.

"Not *because of* that other guy," I say. "But yes, his presence was clarifying, to say the least. How did you know?"

"I knew it from the second I saw that photo of the three of you."

I return to the house my husband and I have shared, and it no longer feels like my home. It no longer feels like the place I want to set roots or start a family. I know I have some logistics to figure out—but my heart has already left this place.

The Dream

IT'S THE TWENTY-SECOND ANNIVERSARY OF MY father's death and I stir from sleep in the early-hour light. It's been a week since my husband and I decided to end our marriage. I am alone, in our house in Todos Santos, pondering my next move. John is back in LA, preparing for his extended work trip, and I'm not sure if I should go with him or if I should use this time to sort out my life on my own.

While my heart and body feel open and ready to receive him, part of me still feels afraid. Afraid I might be moving too quickly. Afraid I could get hurt. Afraid this is all too good to be true. Afraid that ending one relationship and immediately starting another is a recipe for disaster. Afraid that blowing up my life might all blow up in my face.

"Don't rush into this," cautious voices offered. "You barely know him," one person said. "Are you sure you don't want to give your marriage one last go?" a well-meaning friend suggested.

My ex has been swinging between acceptance and denial, and just yesterday he sent me a barrage of text messages saying that *rage is visiting him in a serious way at the suddenness of how this is all unfolding* and that he wants to grow from this experience and fight for our marriage. Reading his words feels like a knife piercing my heart. I hate that he's hurting, but one thing I'm sure of is that I no longer want to be with him. It pains me to write those words to him, but I'm learning, over and over again, that telling the truth is the kindest thing, even when it hurts.

As I lie in bed, eyes closed, somewhere between sleep and consciousness, my father and John's father appear before me suddenly like in a dream. John's father is sitting on a rocking chair while my father is sitting on a bench next to him, stringing a guitar.

"We found each other on the other side," John's dad tells me. "We've been working for some time to bring you and John together. So don't worry—this is all part of the plan. Everything will be more than okay, you'll see."

A single tear slides down my cheek, slowing my thoughts and worries.

"Don't be afraid, my girl. This is what's best for all three of you," my father adds. "Keep leading from your heart. Keep trusting yourself. That is the only way forward."

Even in my sleepy, half-conscious state, I know he's right. I know I'm ready. I know this is everything I've ever longed for and more. I know that my fear of things moving too quickly is more connected to my fear of what other people will think than my own true desires.

I direct my attention at John's dad and say, "I'm so in love with your son. I didn't know it was possible to feel this way. He's the most extraordinary person I've ever known."

"I know," he says, smiling. "So do me a favor, and keep telling him. I know you can love him in the way I once did."

I wake up a few hours later to the sound of my phone buzzing, the conversation with our dads still whispering in my ears.

I look at my phone, squinting as my eyes adjust to the light. It's John.

I had the wildest vision of our fathers this morning during a massage, he says in a text. *Call me when you wake up.*

I shoot up in bed and FaceTime John immediately. "I cannot believe you just texted me that," I say the second he answers. "I'm literally shaking. I had a vision of our dads too. They told me that they found each other in spirit land. And get this, your dad told me—"

"That he chose you to love me in the way he once did?"

⇒⋅⇐

LATER I FACETIME MY mom to tell her about the dream.

She rolls her eyes at my dad's presence. "Why does he get to be the wise one?!"

I roll my eyes back. "Mom, you're missing the point."

"Okay, fine," she says begrudgingly. "Tell me this: If things don't work out with John, would you go back to your ex?"

"No, definitely not." I know this in my bones.

"Then pack your shit and go," she says. "What the hell are you waiting for?"

My mom isn't who I usually turn to for love advice, but this time she is spot on. What am I still doing here? I really should pack my shit and go.

I call John back and say, "I think I should come now."

He says, "Yes, I think you should come now too. I just wanted you to make that decision for yourself."

"What should I do with all my things?"

"Bring as much as you can carry," he says. "We'll figure out later how to get the rest."

And just like that: I'm moving to Los Angeles. I'll figure out what's next from there.

Before We Go
Any Further

IT WOULD BE EASY TO STOP THE STORY HERE. Woman meets soulmate and replaces husband with said man. Some call her reckless, others call her brave. Either way, she lives happily ever after.

But this isn't that kind of story.

An unfulfilling marriage and a chance meeting may have been my wake-up call, but another man's love wasn't going to save me. As I was about to learn the hard way, this isn't the story of woman being saved by Prince Charming. This is the story of a woman learning to save *herself.*

Part 2

Be Brave

Desire

TWENTY-FOUR HOURS AFTER I DECIDED TO MOVE to LA, I packed my entire life into two suitcases and set off.

John and I had committed our lives to each other, but we'd never even kissed. He had yet to brush his hand across the small of my back; I had yet to press my lips to the nape of his neck. We had never seen each other naked. The fact that I hadn't felt desired by a man in years was equal parts thrilling and terrifying. Being in a sexless marriage for so many years was heartbreaking and frustrating, but it was also safe and convenient.

The truth is, I'd been guarding my heart since I was young. As a girl, I shied away from the boys I had feelings for and I never dared speak those feelings aloud. I believed that if a boy knew how I felt about him, he would lose interest. Somewhere along the way, I turned off my desire. It was too scary to want. It wasn't safe to long for someone who might not feel the same and would eventually leave anyway. Instead I chose boys I liked but never loved. Boys who adored me and were more invested in the relationship than I was. This made me feel safe. This gave me control, power, and peace. This ensured that the leaving would happen on my terms.

In my early twenties, booze and Adderall gave me the confidence to test this theory. I strayed from safety and followed the rapture of desire, hoping *Maybe it'll be different this time.* . . . But I had a penchant for choosing emotionally unavailable men who'd break up with me over text, tell me they loved me only to never speak those words again, or hide the fact that even though we'd spent every single day together, they happened to have a girlfriend overseas.

All of these scenarios served only as proof that I was indeed unlovable, unwanted, and flawed—that something was clearly wrong with me. Rather than see their behavior as a reflection of them and not me, and instead of looking inwardly at how chasing unavailability pointed to my own fears of intimacy—it only intensified my belief that love and desire were not to be trusted.

But when I met John, I was suddenly alive with desire.

And this time, the desire felt different. This wasn't the kind of desire that played games or longed for something it couldn't have. This was the kind of desire that burned like a warm, steady flame.

But because it felt so new and foreign, it was also the kind of desire that unsteadied me.

On the flight to LA, I tried to center myself. I knew John and I had the ingredients for strong and lasting love—emotional honesty, depth, respect, trust, and attunement. But what about my inexperience in the bedroom? A sexless marriage hadn't exactly prepared me for this. I flipped through movies, looking for something lighthearted to watch. I mindlessly turned the pages of the in-flight magazine, hoping to pass the time. I picked up my pen, searching for words I couldn't find. The silence only turned up the volume in my head, one thought on repeat: *Do you even know how to make love to a man?* And even more urgently: *If you can't satisfy John, will he still want to be with you?*

I felt annoyed to be thinking these thoughts. I'd just blown up my life, liberated myself from so many "good girl" stories, and now I was en route to John. I wanted to feel joyous and carefree. I wanted to feel bold and fearless. But instead I was haunted by old abandonment stories and not-good-enough insecurities that I thought I'd already healed.

The voice of my friend Vienna kept ringing in my mind:

Any place of activation is a gift. It's putting you back into contact with something that's unresolved—a place you're not yet free.

It's true: I did not feel sexually free. And from what I gathered, John was *very* free, which left me feeling like a virgin schoolgirl who'd never been touched. Though we felt like equals in every other area of our lives, the bedroom was the one place I feared I didn't measure up. When I mentioned this to John, he seemed surprised that the woman who he perceived to be so self-assured was actually stewing in self-doubt, but he responded with gentleness and reassurance. "We have nothing to worry about in that department," he said. "Trust me."

I tried my damnedest to believe him.

The plane landed early at LAX and I texted John the moment I had service. *I'm here*, I said. *So am I*, he replied. I put my phone away, deboarded the plane, and collected my things at baggage claim. I fussed with my dress, fluffed my hair, sucked on a mint, and put on ChapStick. I walked outside, my heart beating out of my chest, finding it hard to catch a deep breath.

John stood in front of his 1991 Saab convertible, a dusty-colored bouquet of flowers in hand, smiling. He wore a simple gray Henley, well-worn cuffed pants, striped socks, and desert boots. I looked into his eyes and he into mine, unwavering. My mind quieted for the first time that day. Each step toward him felt like slow motion—I was releasing the woman I'd known myself to be so I could step into the one I'd always wanted to become.

When he wrapped his arms around me, our bodies softened. I felt my heart and his heart beating at once—our chests colliding and confiding in each other. He turned my head up toward his and placed his lips upon mine. And we kissed. A rush of warmth surged through me, starting at our lips and reaching into every corner of my being. The frenetic pace of the airport became a distant hum; it was just the two of us, wrapped in our own world, together.

"I told you we'd have no problem," he said, his eyes smiling.

He opened my door, and I slipped inside like I'd sat in this seat a thousand times before. We left LAX and headed toward Manhattan Beach, where the sun is warm and the air is salty. We drove along the coast, hand in hand, my heart racing every time he pulled over to brush the hair away from my face, or kiss my eyes, cheeks, and lips, or look at me intently.

I looked back at him with an ache that felt ancient—an ache that never knew it could feel like this. What *this* was exactly, I struggled to put into words. But maybe this feeling didn't need words. Perhaps that's the whole point. Maybe it was the simple knowing that, after thirty-five years of choosing love that was safe yet unfulfilling, or desirous yet unattainable, it was possible to find a love that was both.

Safe *and* extraordinary.

Hunger

LATER THAT EVENING WE PARK IN FRONT OF John's home and share a sweet, tart, couple-glasses-of-wine kiss. He gets out of the car and walks around to open my door, then reaches for my hand. Inside, we take off our shoes and stand in the hall, facing each other. He looks at me with eyes that say *I want you*. I don't know how to look at him with eyes that say *I want you*, but I try. He leads me into the bedroom. We embrace, breathing each other in, pulses quickening.

John leans back to take me in, placing a warm palm on my right cheek. I rest there for a little while. He kisses my neck, unties my dress, and unfastens my bra with the precision and presence that makes me feel like one of his art pieces. I slide my panties down and stand in front of him, naked. "My god," he says. "You are *so* beautiful." His words calm me.

He takes off his shirt, pants, and socks, revealing a figure as chiseled and defined as a real-life *David*. "And so are you," I say, blushing. I want to touch him, but I'm not sure how and I'm afraid I'll do it wrong. So I just stand there, arms pinned to my sides, trying not to look awkward.

Do I know what I'm doing?

I feel out of touch, out of practice, and keenly aware of the experience mismatch between us. Either he can't tell that I'm questioning myself, or he's being kind. He grabs hold of me, guides me to the bed, lowers me to the pillow with strength and grace.

It's a bit of a blur at first. All the stimulation and buildup makes me feel like I'm floating outside my body. It's intense—this desire to please him but not knowing how. *Am I doing okay? Is he enjoying himself? What if I can't measure up? What if I make a fool of myself? What if, what if, what if . . .*

I'm lying on the bed, motionless, frozen like a deer in headlights. I open my eyes amid my swirling thoughts and find John's eyes staring into mine, his desire apparent.

Shhhh, I tell myself. *Be present. Relax into this.*

Beneath my anxious mind, my racing thoughts, my not-enough stories, a feeling rises in me:

Hunger.

I don't know if I've ever felt this before, but I like it very much. I sink into the sensations, and the present moment finds me again. It feels *good* to want and be wanted. To find this hunger alive within me. But . . .

Is John attracted to my body type?

Am I too soft?

How am I supposed to move?

I open my eyes again, and John's loving gaze calms me. I exhale deeply. I'm trying to quiet the what-ifs and let my body lead, but the insecurities swirl. I wonder if he can see how unsure I am—how much I'm second-guessing myself—and if that will change the way he looks at me.

John brushes my hair away from my face and whispers, "You're stunning."

For a moment, I want to believe him. For a moment, I almost do. But the voice in my head is louder.

If you can't satisfy John, why would he want to be with you?

Under the Sheets

IT'S A HUGE RELIEF WHEN JOHN SEEMS TO BE less focused on how I can satisfy *him*, and more intent on how he can satisfy *me*. My face has never been adorned with so many kisses. My body has never been held, caressed, and savored with this much attention and delight. I can no longer keep count of the number of times he's told me that I'm beautiful, and how in love with me he is. A younger version of me would have questioned if his behavior was too good to be true, too loving to trust. But with John, nothing feels like a line—his words come out because he can't help saying them.

Even though I can't remember the last time I've been touched like this, and even though I'm still learning how to connect with my primal, sexual self, all this time under the sheets is certainly helping me to relax into myself—and my inexperience.

But then, one evening, John is flipping through old photos on his phone, trying to find a book he wants me to read. I nuzzle my head into his shoulder while we browse through his history. A photo appears and renders me motionless. It's a very sexy, very petite woman, naked on a bed, ready to be taken. I stop breathing and let out an audible gasp.

"I'm so sorry you had to see that," he says, wrapping his arms around me and kissing my forehead. He holds his lips there for a moment, probably avoiding eye contact, but also giving me space to process and collect myself. I start breathing again. He deletes the photo and then asks, "Are you okay?"

I don't look like that. I don't know how to be sexy like that. I can't compete with that.

I can't find my words, so he continues. "I'll go through and delete anything else like that. But I hope you know there is nowhere I'd rather be than in this moment with you." I hear him, and believe him, but it's too late. My mind is already spinning a web of fear, wondering how on earth I could ever measure up to the petite models, famous actresses, and sexually liberated women he's dated. I'm still trying to reconnect with my sexual self—and this is what I'm up against? *I don't know how to seduce a man. This is way out of my league.*

I receive John's reassurance and try to brush off the incident. He asks me several times if I'm okay, and I tell him that I'm fine. I can tell he knows I'm *not* fine, but I don't yet know how to express what's brewing inside me. I excuse myself to take a shower, closing the door behind me. I take off my clothes and look in the mirror. I turn around and pop my butt up in the air, trying on my best sexy face. *Hey, big boy,* I mouth. I walk toward the mirror slowly while grabbing my breasts. "Come and get me," I whisper. *This is ridiculous,* I think, embarrassed, exhaling sharply and rolling my eyes. *I look like a damn fool. I'm not sexy enough, thin enough, or experienced enough.*

I grab my phone and text a friend.

I don't even know how to touch John!!! What am I supposed to do with his penis???

Hahahaha, she texts back immediately. *You just . . . GRAB IT!!!* I laugh loudly and for a brief moment experience relief.

I get into the shower and close my eyes under the warm water, hoping to calm my thoughts.

Instead one thought rises above the rest: *What if he changes his mind about me?*

Performance Anxiety

A FEW WEEKS AGO, WHEN IT WAS JUST ME, MY vibrator, and my imagination, I casually mentioned to John that I "come quickly," which I've since come to regret. Had I considered how that simple statement might create pressure and performance anxiety, I wouldn't have said a word.

Sure, when I was alone, lusting for him, it didn't take much. But add in all the stimulation, newness, and *Am I enough?* inner dialogue, and an orgasm has felt out of reach.

I'm trying to be present. I'm trying to get out of my head and into my body. I'm trying to let go. But I can't get the photograph of that sexy woman out of my mind. As John is pleasuring me, I keep seeing flashes of her and her perfectly petite body. *Is that his type? Did they have better sex? Is that the kind of seduction he's used to?* After a long while between my legs and . . . nothing, John asks, with a touch of frustration, "What do you want, my love?"

"You inside me," I say.

We move from position to position until I'm on the edge of the bed, hungry for more. "Show me how you touch yourself," he says. I oblige, turned on by his direction.

My breath quickens as I lower my hand, feeling the heat of

his gaze on me. His eyes are intense, watching every movement, every reaction, heightening my arousal and making me feel both exposed and wanted. He moves closer, his breath hot against my ear as he whispers, "That's it. Just like that." My mind finally starts to quiet as I feel every sensation more acutely—the warmth of his body, the soft rustling of the sheets beneath me, and the intoxicating scent of our mingled sweat and desire. He slides himself back inside of me.

I close my eyes, tilt my head back, grab hold of the sheets, and moan.

Finally.

As I lie there, feeling raw and vulnerable and tingly, John kisses me. Eventually he gets up from bed and walks into the bathroom. He turns on the shower and gets inside. "Can we make a pact?" he calls out a few minutes later. "Let's be honest and fully transparent about any and all insecurities that arise for us, no matter how hard it might be to say them out loud. There's nothing to be ashamed of, ever, as long as we don't keep it bottled up. What do you think?"

"I love that," I call back. "Can I start now?" I say, laughing.

He turns off the shower and swings open the curtain. "Talk to me," he says playfully, his naked body dripping with water.

I tilt back my head and erupt into laughter.

"I'm waiting," he says.

I pause briefly to consider my words, my throat tightening. "This feels really vulnerable to voice," I start, clearing my throat. "But ever since I saw that picture of that hot little body on that bed, I can't escape the thought that I'm not your type and you may be more attracted to a woman like her. I'm still learning how to connect with my sexual self, and it feels like I have steep competition with the women from your past. So I've been in my head a lot, feeling worried that I won't be able to satisfy you, and scared you might change your mind about me."

I'm relieved to say this out loud, though I'm nervous about how he will respond. I learned at a young age that if I express how I'm really feeling, other people won't be able to handle it. Either they'll have feelings about my feelings, be uncomfortable, call me overly sensitive, or dismiss my emotions as "no big deal." This led me to believe that I need to figure out my feelings alone—that other people can't hold space for me and don't have the skills to do so. It also left me with an uneasy sense of shame for desiring comfort and reassurance.

I'm surprised when John's response doesn't follow the pattern I've come to expect. Instead he comes and sits next to me, placing his hand on my cheek. "I totally understand why that would make you feel that way, and again, I'm so sorry you had to see that," he says, his eyes not leaving mine. And then slowly and calmly, as if he wants every word to land, he continues, "I love you more than I've ever loved anyone. I love your body and beautiful curves. There's a reason I'm not with any of the women from my past. I choose you. We're still learning each other, and it takes time, so this is all very normal."

My jaw relaxes and my breath deepens. It feels safe to be seen for who I truly am. The more emotionally naked I get, the closer we can become. He keeps showing me that he's here, as my partner, to safely navigate the insecurities that come up in building something good and true.

"How does that feel?" he asks.

"So much better," I say, reaching for his hand.

"And I'm glad you brought this up," he adds. "Because I was going to share that I was feeling a touch insecure about all this talk of you coming so damn quickly," he says with a chuckle. "But now I think I understand where that was coming from."

"Oh yeah?" I say.

"Oh yeah," he echoes back, leaning in to tickle me. I kick out my legs and tilt my head back, laughing, our bodies intertwined like thread.

Soapgate

I WOULDN'T EXACTLY CONSIDER MYSELF TRADI-
tional "wife material." I don't cook. I don't clean. I leave
cups around the apartment, which John stacks up, and with
a hair of frustration, he sighs: "You are a messy roommate,
you know that?"

I was raised by an entrepreneurial mom who taught me
how to make money when I was five, build computers when
I was six, and pass out work orders to her all-male team
when I was nine. I can run a business, motivate a team, and
speak onstage in front of thousands of people, but put my
dishes in the sink? That one always seems to slip my mind.

John knew I was domestically challenged before we
moved in together, but now that we're living in a six-hundred-
square-foot apartment in Venice Beach, I think the reality is
starting to set in. For both of us.

John is precise. Immaculate, even. Every single piece of
art and decor has a place. His shirts, socks, and pants are
folded using a specific method. He uses a toothbrush to gently clean the leaves of the many plants that adorn the windows. While it certainly contributes to creating a beautiful
space, I'm starting to feel like I'm getting on his nerves with

my clothes, dishes, and journals strewn about. And if I'm honest, he's starting to get on mine too.

"My love, that's not how you wash a dish," he'll instruct. "You didn't even get all the food off."

While some people might find this advice-giving helpful, I find it rather annoying. Did I mention that I hate being told what to do?

One morning, when he's about to jump in the shower, he points to a bar of soap I put in the dish on the bathroom counter. "What's this?"

"A bar of soap," I say.

"But there's the same bar of soap under it," he says.

"Yeah, but it's almost gone."

"But why didn't you finish the first one before opening the new one?"

Somehow, soap talk quickly escalates into yelling and then, before we know it, name-calling.

"You're so wasteful," he laments.

"Leave me alone; you're always nagging me," I say in defense. "Everything is *your* way," I say. "What if *I* have a way too?"

"You have *no* way!"

I storm out of the room, slam the door, and scream, "I don't think we're compatible!"

Is our big, beautiful love story really about to be blown up by a bar of soap?

The Therapist

I WENT INTO MY RELATIONSHIP WITH JOHN thinking that since I've healed so much past trauma, our love story was going to be a breeze. But it turns out that while I've intellectually understood and become aware of much of my trauma, I have not actually *processed* it. Because anytime we edge toward an uncomfortable conversation— even about soap—I shut down, need to leave the room, and feel physically unsteady. I start questioning whether we're compatible and if something's wrong with the relationship. Even small moments of conflict can have me mentally packing my bags and ready to leave. Knowing that I do not, in fact, want to pack my bags and leave, inspires me to seek out a new therapist.

I click a link on my computer to find my therapist, Christine, in our Zoom room. "Hey, Amber," she says, with kind eyes and a soothing voice that relaxes my whole nervous system.

For the first thirty minutes or so, I give her the bullet points to get her up to speed on the last few months of my life. Eventually, things get interesting.

"I understand how all this change would feel like a lot to navigate," she says reassuringly. "And I'm curious, if you had to sum up in one sentence what brought you here today, what would it be?"

"Well, to put it simply, I'm all in on my relationship and I'm afraid it's going to go away."

"What does that fearful part of you think she needs to do to keep John close?" she asks.

She thinks she has to be perfect and she can't mess up.

She thinks she has to be a good girl and she can't cause any trouble.

She thinks she has to take care of herself, never expressing needs or asking for help.

She thinks she has to be happy all the time and isn't allowed to have "negative" feelings.

She thinks she has to be thin, sexy, and perfectly put together.

She thinks she always has to be solid, wise, enlightened, and evolved.

"And if you don't keep this up, then what happens?"

"He leaves," I say, my eyes wet with tears.

"Oh, Amber," Christine says. "That feels like *a lot* of pressure. Do you feel that?"

Having lost my voice somewhere, I nod.

"Do you see how any sign of John being frustrated or disappointed could have you thinking you need to pack up your bags—before he does?"

I nod again.

Christine invites me to name the age that's associated with all of my fearful parts. The perfectionist is six; the happy part is nine. The thin part is twelve and the solid one is sixteen. As I do this, I realize that my wise adult self is not afraid of love and intimacy; it's the young, vulnerable parts I

105

buried a long time ago that are now rearing their heads and trying to protect me. These parts believe love is conditional and I have to please, perform, and be perfect to be deserving and worthy of love. It's these parts that led me to suffer silently with an eating disorder for ten years—*If I'm thin, I'm lovable*—and an Adderall addiction for five—*If I'm achieving, I'm worthy.* I harmed myself to feel in control, to feel enough, but mostly to feel worthy of love.

But now my adult self knows better. And I'm ready to heal. I'm ready to look honestly at my past and revisit the stories that are keeping me small. I'm ready to believe that I'm worthy of love just as I am—imperfect and flawed.

Christine guides me to close my eyes, take a deep breath, and let the young parts of me know that they don't have to protect me anymore. "You're safe now," I tell them.

And so our work begins.

⇥⇤

I GET HOME FROM therapy and talk to John. We apologize to each other for getting worked up over something as inconsequential as soap. And knowing that we weren't actually arguing about soap—but about our values, preferences, and needs—we share, we listen, we go deeper. Argument by argument, we learn more about how we can take care of each other—how we help each other feel safe and seen. Slowly, I begin to realize that conflict doesn't mean incompatibility. Resolving these little spats by coming back together and taking responsibility for our roles shows me that it's safe to open up about the big things too.

I go into the bathroom later that day and laugh to myself when I see that John has thrown the old soap in the trash.

Thanks for Checking In

I'M GETTING A MASSAGE. THE PRESSURE IS TOO light, and the massage therapist won't stop talking. I want to tell her that I like a firmer touch and I need quiet to relax, but I don't speak up. I'm afraid I'll offend or disappoint her.

"So her comfort is more important than your enjoyment?" Christine asks a few days later.

Oof.

If my fear of disappointing a massage therapist has me feeling this uncomfortable, you can imagine my reaction when people start hearing about John and me, and that I'm no longer with my husband. The rumor mill is in full swing, and people have strong opinions and big feelings about all of it.

I can't believe you left your marriage for another man.
Heartless. Home-wrecker. Horrible person.
This is not what people with character do.
You don't even know this guy. You can't possibly be in love yet.
I don't want to be part of your PR campaign.
Prove it; make a case for love.

People share those thoughts with me or with friends of

Amber Rae

mine or, in one case, with a first date who happens to be friends with a friend of mine. These judgments are unsolicited, to say the least, and they make me wonder what my ex-husband is telling people in our shared community.

As much as I tell myself not to care and that people's perspectives have little to do with me—I find myself caring very much, defending my position, and wanting to explain my side of things to people who are supposed to be my friends. People I've known for years, who I thought would say with compassion, "How are you doing? I know this must be a lot to navigate," surprise me when they instead question my character and choices, even if they don't know the full story.

Initially I think that if I can help them understand—if I can give them the play-by-play, prove John is my person, and that my ex and I were not the right fit—their narrative of me will change, they won't see me as the villain, and I will feel better. But the more I explain myself, the worse I feel.

One night, while wallowing in the judgments of others, John big-spoons his arms around me and says:

"I know it's disappointing how some people are responding to our news. It must feel really shitty. But in these moments, just try to remember that people search their entire lives for a love like this. We found it. We know what this is. We're so blessed to have found each other. And that's all that really matters. Some people will understand and embrace us, and others won't. But you're okay no matter what—remember that. People can feel however they want to feel, and the way they respond will help us determine who we want to be close with moving forward."

This perspective comes in handy a few days later when an

old friend catches me off guard by saying, "You can't possibly fall in love this quickly."

As I furrow my brow, retract my body, and look at him like *Huh?*, he jumps in. "Remember our joke about you having flavors of the week when you were living in New York in your twenties?" he asks.

"Are you seriously referring to a few guys I dated well over a decade ago when I was a twentysomething single woman?" I respond. "My only regret from that period of my life is not dating *more*. And what does that have to do with anything?"

"I just wonder if this is like that and you don't really know how you feel yet."

I look at him with eyes that say *Seriously?* and then I laugh. I mean, *laugh* laugh, like a bell is ringing from the top of my head to the pit of my belly.

"Well, prove it then," he says. "Make a case for love."

I could say that love doesn't need a case. Love isn't something we bring into a courtroom and debate; it's something we feel in our bones. I could say that your need for me to make a case for love tells me more about your relationship with love than mine. I could say that when two people are open to the giving and receiving of love, without limits or constraints, you transcend into oneness together. That's what it means to say "I love you." The divine in me recognizes the divine in you. You are not the source of my love; I am not the source of your love. We are mirrors through which love reflects and awakens. I could say that love with a capital L challenges you to step up, to rise, to become more of who you actually are. I could say that I know it's love because I Know, and that's enough—

But instead I say, "My love for John needs no proof or explanation. But thanks for checking in."

Shame

ONE DAY DURING THE SEPARATION, MY PHONE rings and it's my ex calling out of the blue. Nervously, I answer, my pacing footsteps echoing through the living room.

"My world is shattered," he says, catching me off guard. "Relationships go through ebbs and flows. Intimacy goes through ebbs and flows. But we had a foundation to work with. I feel tossed to the side and not considered. You didn't make it clear that you were unhappy. You made a rash decision and you left me for another man without a dialogue."

You left me for another man.

As those six words come into focus, shame enters like a stampede of horses. A choir echoes in my mind in unison: *Bad girl!* I step into the arena, ready to fight. "Have you considered that you'd already left?" I say, my voice rising with each word. "You were always distracted, always working, not available. And without a dialogue? Please! You were *part* of the dialogue. And let's take John out of this. All of these issues existed before he came into the picture. We were avoiding them!"

"Well, you got John, so I think it's fair that I get the land," he says. And there it is—a subtle attempt to guilt me into giving him what he wants.

"Seriously?" I ask, holding a chair to steady myself. Later I will realize that how my ex feels about our relationship ending has nothing to do with how we resolve the land. These are fundamentally separate issues. But right now I'm at a loss for words, shame galloping through me, wild and untamed.

"Well, I'm still fighting for us," he says. "And I'm the one out here trying to protect you and your reputation."

"My reputation?" I say, my blood boiling. I hang up the phone, lean against the wall, and fall to the ground, tears streaming down my face.

This guilt feels . . . hauntingly familiar.

Trained in Tolerance

I'M TWELVE YEARS OLD, ON SPRING BREAK. I'M walking down a sidewalk, staring at my sneakers, my stomach rolling in circles. My mom and stepdad are walking quickly up ahead, and yelling at each other loudly. He's babbling about something, but he's so drunk, I can barely understand him through his slurring. In his hands, he's shaking the keys to our car with a glint of rage in his eyes—a sound I can still hear to this day. I look up ahead—we're walking toward the parking lot. I feel so panicked, I can barely breathe. I think: *This is how my dad died.*

"I'm not getting in the car," I yell. "You can't drive." My stepdad raises his arms and roars like a bear. My mom starts yelling back. I can tell I just made things worse.

They keep yelling—at each other, and then at me. My stepdad's words are mumbled, but his anger is sharp. "Get in the car!" he bellows, barely audible through his drunken haze. My mom shouts something back, but I can't hear her over the pounding in my chest.

What do I do, what do I do, what do I do? I think, scanning the environment. I see a police officer ahead and a wave of relief rushes over me. As I move toward the cop, saying,

"They can't drive. Can you please tell them not to drive?" my mom screams, "STOP!" in tandem. She pulls on my step-dad's shirt, he pulls away, the shirt rips.

"Ma'am, is everything all right?" the police officer asks my mom, walking toward her.

"Amber! Get over here!" my mom yells, yanking my arm hard.

Before I can understand what's happening, the officer is placing handcuffs around my mom's wrists, telling her that she has the right to remain silent. She looks at me with pure venom as she gets into the back seat of the police car. A small crowd has formed. People are staring.

Oh no, I think, and my mind goes somewhere blank and far away that is hard to name.

"Look at what you did," my stepdad slurs.

→ ·←

I'M TWENTY-THREE YEARS OLD, back home in Chicago for the Fourth of July. I live in San Francisco now and work for a tech start-up. I left my hometown six months ago to chase my dreams, take some risks, and get a fresh start of my own—but mostly I needed to get away from all the family drama.

I'm showing my mom my new iPhone when a notification pops up on the screen, making my body freeze. My stepdad, or *ex*-stepdad as I like to call him these days, just emailed me . . . again. I walk into the other room and hold my breath.

Today marks six years since I've seen you last, he says, piercing through the armor I try so hard to wear. *Heard you moved out of state but never said goodbye?* He tells me he loves me like his own child but I tossed him aside—abandoning him without explanation. *I want you in my life,* he goes on, *but you need to be ALL in with me. I cannot handle more disappointment and broken hearts from you. It's never too late to say you're sorry . . .*

I lean against the wall and fall to the ground, my stomach twisting into knots. This is the same man who was soothed by two things: a cold can of beer and holding me. When I was ten years old, he'd cuddle me in bed like I was a comfort object—*his* teddy bear. When my mom hollered for him to get out of my bedroom, NOW, he'd whisper for me to call her "Old Yeller." As I got older, I'd overhear him joke with his friends about my "great ass." He'd scream at me when he couldn't find his hairbrush, only to discover he'd placed it in the wrong drawer. And somehow, he blamed me for his drunken stupor and my mom's arrest during that spring break trip all those years ago.

Yet, still, I feel guilty, like I owe him something. I place my head in my hands and let the tears flow.

⇒⋅⇐

AM I THE ONE who leaves—who tosses people to the side? I write at the top of a fresh page in my journal, thirty-five years old now and still haunted by what feels like ancient guilt. *I thought I was the one who overstayed.* I tap my finger against a page, lips pursed. *Which one is it?*

I place my journal next to me and call Vienna. She's a marriage and family therapist but she's also my friend, so I trust her to cut through the bullshit and give it to me straight.

"Am I the one who leaves or am I the one who overstays?" I ask her without saying hello.

She laughs lovingly. "What's going on?"

"I've been feeling a lot of shame about how I left my marriage," I say. "But I'm realizing my shame isn't just about my ex; it's also connected to the guilt I feel for abandoning my ex-stepdad."

"Do you need me to tell you that you didn't abandon your stepdad?" she asks.

"Maybe," I say, my voice squeaking, a nervous laugh rumbling through me like I'm back in my sixteen-year-old body.

"Okay, well, you did *not* abandon him," she emphasizes. "You made a choice to leave a relationship that was abusive."

Abusive.

That word hangs in the air. *Was his behavior abusive?* I ask myself. *Is that what that was? Wouldn't it be dramatic to label it that way? Was it really that bad? Wasn't it also sometimes good?*

"Yeah, I think my little girl was confused because sometimes he was reliable and kind, and other times he was awful and cruel, so I believed that was normal," I say.

"It wasn't normal," Vienna says. "It was normalized."

In my body her words ring true.

"You learned to withstand and tolerate a lot," she reflects. "With your stepdad, it was his inappropriate behavior. With your ex, it was his invulnerability and disconnection.

"And when we tolerate, we have to become very convincing. We have to bargain with our minds, saying, *Well, he has a really big project, and everything will be okay on the other side.* Or, *Once we're married, it'll be better.*"

"Right," I say. "Is that why I was always asking—*How do I make this work? How do I figure this out?* And then I was making plans and taking steps toward that, oblivious to my own true needs."

"Exactly," she says. "That's why even today it's hard for you to say it's abuse with your stepdad. That's a very hard thing to say, you know? And you had to make it *not* that to maintain the relationship. But your pain needs to be honored. Your story needs to be acknowledged. You do that by labeling it accurately rather than tiptoeing around it."

"Oof," I say, her words like a key turning in a long-locked door.

"And with your ex, it was: *How do I tolerate you being so disconnected? How do I tolerate you being so far away from me? How do I tolerate my loneliness? How do I tolerate all of these things?* You were deeply trained in tolerance."

Trained in tolerance. That phrase stands out like an ad in the paper from the 1950s: *Looking for women blind to their own needs & trained in tolerance.* I chuckle at this thought, and then ask, "So how do I tolerate less?"

"You're already doing it," she says. "As you're stepping into your authenticity, you're losing people and relationships are changing, which is all very normal. The healthy part of tolerance is being able to tolerate the outcomes and consequences of you living authentically. So instead of tolerating bad behavior, disconnection, and so on, you learn to tolerate the discomfort of someone being disappointed in you or someone feeling hurt as a result of your choices. And that doesn't mean we have to be savages, of course. We can allow someone's hurt to touch us. We can care about people's experiences—just not at the expense of our own."

You Heal in All Directions

A FEW DAYS LATER, AFTER SHARING MY SHAME revelations with Christine, she asks, "Would you say leaving your marriage was the highest good for all?"

"Absolutely—without question."

"So the way I see it—you didn't do anything wrong. Instead you made things right. John helped make the lack, limitations, and denial visible and conscious. And once you saw reality accurately, you did what was most true. No one likes to pull the plug, but if a relationship is on life support, letting it suffer is no good. Leaving the relationship is an act of mercy—it allows both people to find what's most fulfilling before they resent and hate each other."

"That all makes sense, but why do I still feel shame for being the one who left?" I ask.

"What does shame sound like to you?" she asks. "What does shame say?"

"I'm a bad girl. I hurt people. I can't believe you left your marriage for another man."

"What does being bad serve in this moment?" she asks with laser precision.

"Good question," I say. "I guess that by holding on to shame, by focusing on my being bad, I don't get to be fully present with John. I've gotten everything I've always wanted, but now I'm too guilty to enjoy it."

"There it is," she says. "So you're punishing yourself. Do you think that carrying the shame is also a way of showing your ex and other people that you care?"

"Maybe, yeah . . ." I say. "That also feels true."

"Why do you think you want people to know that you care so much?"

"I think I'm trying to protect myself from being seen as the villain," I say. "If I care and if I'm hurting too, maybe people won't see me as the bad guy."

"That's very honest," she says. "And there's also room here to get a whole lot more nuanced so that you're part of the story. Yes, your actions hurt your ex, but you also don't just hurt people and you are not a bad person because you left a relationship. You were also trying really hard to get your needs met for a long time."

"That's true," I say, exhaling deeply. "I wonder if this is intensified for me because I come from a lineage of women who were left by their men in really painful ways. Like, how dare I do what was done to them? Now *I'm* the villain in the family line."

"I hear that," she says. "And you also have to realize that there's a lot of generational healing in the fact that you left. I imagine that a lot of these women should have left or wanted to leave but, because of the times, didn't have the financial resources or emotional strength to do so. I don't want you to disregard the very real healing and reclamation that's occurring for the women in your line. I imagine if we asked most of them, they wouldn't say, *My relationship was amazing*. They probably put up with a lot of things that weren't okay. You had the courage to step into something others didn't know how to do; instead they waited until the man did the leaving in very painful and betraying ways."

"I hadn't considered that," I say, the hairs on the back of my neck standing.

"While what you did could easily be judged by people who can't see a bigger story and likely have their own pain around being left, what you did here is a really big, expansive, courageous thing. There's been this long pattern in your family and you stepped out of it. As they always say, you heal in all directions."

You heal in all directions.

Every time shame comes knocking on my door, I remind myself of this. *You heal in all directions.* I may have been the one who ripped off the bandage, exposing the wound, but that doesn't mean the bandage was meant to stay on. It was going to come off eventually; I'm just the one who pulled it off first. Of course it hurts and is uncomfortable as all hell right now, but the wound is exposed. The wound can breathe.

With time, the wound can heal.

Rocky

GROWING UP, I FELT LIKE I HAD TWO MOTHERS— my grandmother, who was a source of maternal comfort, and my mom, who felt more like a sister. Often, a *younger* sister.

I'd call my grandmother to vent, irritated and flustered. "Mom's being unreasonable."

"Stop calling Gram to get me in trouble," my mom would say later, part annoyed, part playful. Feeling like the adult in the room, I'd roll my eyes at her petulance—a role reversal I didn't yet understand.

My mom was big—larger than life, colorful, and full of elaborate stories. Her emotions could swing wildly, pulling everyone along for the ride. While my mom filled the room with her vibrant, unpredictable energy, my grandmother anchored it with her calm, unwavering stability. I never once heard her raise her voice. She remained grounded during chaotic moments and always stuck to the facts. In a childhood where I could be left wondering, *What the hell is going on?*, she was my safe place—the quiet in the storm.

For most of my childhood, my grandmother lived down the street. On weekends, she'd cook meals and we'd watch *Unsolved Mysteries* together. She'd ask me questions and listen closely as I answered, then share stories about grow-ing up in England. Sometimes we'd dress up and go into the city for a show. Our favorite tradition, though, was watching Miss America. We'd get our scorecards ready and sit side by side on the couch, evaluating the contestants' talent, style, and presence—or, let's be honest, mostly their appearance. We'd compare our scores with the judges' and cheer aloud whenever we came close.

At the time, it felt like harmless fun, but I ache now for the little girl who learned that beauty and perfection were something to rank. Still, what stays with me most is the comfort of being with Gram—how her warm presence felt like being wrapped in a blanket, a safe place where I could just be myself.

My mom once admitted to me that she was jealous of my connection with Gram. At first I thought she was pointing to a gap in our closeness and her desire to feel a deeper bond with me. But she surprised me when she said it was because of how much Gram loved and cared for me in ways she hadn't received herself. It hadn't occurred to me until that moment that my mom was hungry for her mother's love, which made a lot more sense when I learned about Rocky.

"When I was sixteen, your granddad ran a bar and my friend played in one of the bands," my mom told me. "One day that friend casually mentioned running into my dad and his girlfriend. 'His girlfriend???' I asked. 'What do you mean?' Since Gram was always sweeping things under the rug, I went home and told her to get in the car—*now*. We drove to the bar, and sure enough, when we got there, he was with another woman. Gram was completely distraught and shouted, 'Get her, Beverly, get her!' So I walked over there and punched her in the face. And, well . . . that's how I got the nickname Rocky." As she said those final words, her face lit up and her voice filled with pride.

I remember taking in this story with wide eyes and a sense of *So that's why you're the way you are*. It wasn't until much later that I realized what had really happened that day:

My grandma didn't have a protector, so she turned to my mom to play the part. My mom, a child, got into a physical altercation with an adult woman—all to protect her mother from her adulterous father and, more than anything, to protect herself. Desperate for safety and stability, my mom stepped in without hesitation to fight Gram's battle for her. I imagine she believed, *If my mom can't take care of herself, I'll do it for her. That way, I'll be taken care of too*. My heart breaks thinking about the fear and adrenaline coursing through her young body—a child in a grown-up world. Nothing more.

From that moment on, my mom and Gram's lives became bound together. My granddad eventually married the girl-friend, and my mom's boyfriend moved in to help pay bills and offer support. Later Gram became the office manager of my mom's thriving construction business, a role my mom created to help her live a good life. Every event, every holiday—even when my granddad was hosting with his wife—my mom en-sured Gram was invited to be there. I can't remember a life event she wasn't part of. While I loved having Gram around and never questioned it, I imagine my mom thought being a "good daughter" meant taking care of her mother by includ-ing her in everything and being fiercely loyal to her—even when it came at the expense of herself.

I always got the sense my mom wanted me to "have her back" in this same way too. While my mom never explicitly asked me to fight her battles for her—she seemed content doing that herself—it felt like she wanted me to take her side no matter what. But that often made me feel uneasy. There were plenty of times I didn't agree with her reactions and choices or how she'd get caught up in other people's business. She was always fighting for or against someone, often bringing into our home people she called "broken wings"— family members or friends who needed a place to stay while they got back on their feet.

"They need me," she'd say, but it was apparent to me she needed them too. The need to be needed motivated my mom, and it felt like her way of proving her worth. But now I realize it was more than that—fighting for others was how she quieted her own hurt, trying to give to others what she longed to receive herself: care and protection.

It's a pattern I now see repeated across generations—each of us trying to protect, to fix, to create safety, even though it wasn't meant to be our job. We learned one thing and we repeated it because it was all we knew, and we never thought to question it.

So what I find myself wondering now is this: When it comes to love, how do I untangle the threads of what's been passed down—so I can learn something new?

Surrogates

ONE DAY, MY EX CALLS UNEXPECTEDLY WHILE I'M driving. I hesitate to answer, but habit wins over and I accept the call. He tells me he's taking a sabbatical from work, is running every day, eating well, down forty pounds, and working with a top therapist who specializes in internal family systems, my favorite body of psychology. "I'm doing everything you always wanted me to do," he says like a boy waiting for his star sticker.

My chest tightens, and my body starts to tremble. I pull over to the side of the road, not sure how I'm supposed to feel about this, let alone how I'm supposed to respond. I go with, "Oh good, I'm so happy for you," but what I also mean is *How disappointing that my love wasn't enough for you to take care of yourself when we were together.*

"Who does that remind you of?" Christine asks a few days later. "Who did you want to take better care of themselves when you were a kid?"

"Oof," I say. "My mom. My dad, too."

"How so?"

"I always wanted my mom to smoke less, drink less, eat better, communicate less aggressively—to address her trauma in healthy ways," I say. "I thought if she really loved me, she would do those things for me. I've been trying to convince her to stop smoking since I was seven."

"And?" Christine asks.

"She still smokes," I say, and we both laugh. "And with my dad, it's more . . . why did you get in a car when you were drunk and high? Why didn't you take care of yourself so you could have taken care of us?"

"It sounds like your ex was a surrogate for your wound with your parents," she says. "No wonder you stayed so long and didn't want to give up. No wonder you cared so much and held on to hope. You were desperately trying to resolve your relationship with your parents through your relationship with your ex. You thought if he could just change, if he could take care of himself and follow through, then he'd be emotionally available and present in your relationship. Your marriage would resolve your early conditioning and you'd finally be safe and okay."

A wave of grief rolls over me. All those years of begging my ex to work less, to take care of his body, to honor his health, to do the inner work—it was never just about him. What I was really asking was this:

Mom, Dad's already gone. Will you take care of yourself so I know you'll still be here to take care of me?

Memories

THERE ARE SO MANY THINGS THAT HAVE happened—some I've forgotten, or maybe I chose to forget. Or maybe some things I forgot simply because I needed to. But lately, I've started to remember. Here are some of those memories, in no particular order:

— Putting magazines in my pants so the spanking wouldn't hurt so bad.
— The thud of a foot trying to kick down my bedroom door.
— The smell of cigarette smoke, thick and suffocating.
— Ducking just in time to miss the punch.
— Waking up alone in the back seat of a car, the word BAR glowing on a neon sign outside the window.
— The heavy silence after a slammed door.
— The hundreds of times I heard Mom's famous last words: "I've only had one drink." Sometimes while slurring, sometimes after I'd seen her refill her glass four times, and sometimes when she'd look at me with glassy eyes and say "What?!" as if I were fooled easily.

Christine looks across at me, with as much care and compassion as a therapist is allowed. "Wow, Amber, it sounds like you had a really unpredictable, chaotic, and sometimes scary childhood."

"It does?" I ask in earnest.

She smiles softly, an almost undetectable nod, a hint of sadness at the outskirts of her eyes.

"There was a lot of good too," I say quickly, grasping it like a lifeline.

"I'm sure there was," she says. "And it's also okay to let yourself see the whole picture."

Where Is My Mother?

WHEN I WAS GROWING UP, MY MOM WAS "THE cool mom." Everyone loved her because she was young and hip and threw the best parties. She let us borrow her makeup, and then she'd ask for our advice on her outfits. She acted like she was one of us, but cooler, taking us to trendy restaurants, dishing out advice, and showing us how to have a good time. My mom was the best, my friends were jealous, and I considered myself lucky.

It wasn't until I left my marriage that this story started to show some cracks. My ex was the convenient poster child of emotional unavailability in my story, but he didn't inflict the original wound. Even though my mom was "the cool mom," she wasn't always the *safe* one. And even though she was always there, always present—often it wasn't in the ways I needed.

She championed my accomplishments, but when it came to the deep stuff—my fears, my struggles, my feelings—she wasn't available in the way I longed for. I could share my successes, but there wasn't space for my pain. Sometimes I wondered if she saw my success as her success and my struggles as her failure. The reality is, I didn't feel close to my mom because I didn't feel seen by her.

Her "work hard, play harder" spirit and tendency to self-medicate with alcohol often meant I had to be the adult in the room. I learned to scan her moods, anticipate her reactions, and step in to calm the chaos before it got out of control. That constant scanning left me anxious, always on edge. I didn't get to just be a kid; I grew up too fast.

Years of her telling me, "You're everything to me . . . the most important thing in my life" and on a few occasions, "The only good thing I have going for me" may have made my little girl feel special and valuable, but more, it made me feel bound to my mother—like I was responsible for her happiness and sense of meaning. Add booze to the equation, and I was constantly on edge in her presence. *Is she okay? Did she drink too much? Is she high? Will she lash out if I say that? Is she upset with me? Did I do something wrong?* And even now, *What will the consequences be when she reads this?*

When I distanced myself from her as an adult—both emotionally and physically—it felt like a betrayal, not a right, even when that distance was essential for my own sanity and well-being.

One night, in the midst of looking more honestly at our relationship, I dream I'm in my childhood home. It's totally destroyed—furniture is flipped over, floors are torn up, walls are crumbling. My ex is hosting a raging party. I'm wearing an oversized tee and I'm trying to get to bed, trying to turn down the music, like I did so many times as a kid. I tell my ex he doesn't live here; everyone at this party needs to go.

He says he's renting space in the basement of the house, so he can throw as many parties as he likes.

Where is my mother? I ask, anxiety rising.

I run upstairs and slip quietly into her room. She's sitting in the corner, hair disheveled, drinking vodka discreetly out of a camcorder, a cigarette burning in the ashtray. She's startled when she sees me, her eyes widening as if caught in the act.

"What's going on?" I say. "Is that vodka you're hiding? This needs to stop, Mom!"

"I can leave," she says nonchalantly, bringing the cigarette to her mouth.

I'm overwhelmed by anxiety, sadness, anger, and a fear of abandonment. Even though my mom is physically here, she is emotionally gone. There is so much I want to say, but no words come.

I wake, one line of the dream repeating:

Where is my mother?

I want to depend on her, I want to trust her, I want to feel safe with her, but I don't. And that makes me really sad.

"Are you aware of your role as your mom's manager?" Christine asks a few days later.

"Sort of," I say.

"You were never responsible for your mother's path, but you made that your role in an attempt to create safety."

"I'm not responsible for my mother's path," I repeat in that session and every time my pleaser, accommodator, fixer, healer, and manager comes online. I repeat it when my mom texts me under the influence, when I watch her put a drink to her lips and my entire body freezes, when she uses guilt to try to get her way. I repeat it when she calls me to emotionally dump, when she dismisses my feelings, when she communicates aggressively, or not at all. I repeat those words when I find myself fantasizing about how she might change and how maybe one day she'll "get it." I repeat those words when she refuses to repair the hurt she's caused.

I just keep repeating *I'm not responsible for my mother's path*, hoping my habitual responses to her will start to shift. Because maybe then I'll stop trying to change her. Maybe I'll stop holding on to the hope that she'll become someone different. That she'll learn to take care of herself, and me, in the ways I long for.

Instead, I let myself feel what's real. What is. I wade into the waters of longing, grief, disappointment, rage, and sorrow. Because I can no longer run from it. I can no longer bend reality into something it so sadly isn't. I just have to feel it, in every fiber of my being. I feel it all, and I cry. And when I'm done crying, all that's left for me to do is take impeccable care of *myself*, the care I've always longed for. I cook myself a healthy meal. I move my body. I go to therapy. I journal about my feelings. I rest when I'm tired. Everything I wish my mother would do for herself, and everything I wish she would have done for me, I do it for myself instead.

She can be a painful mirror but a powerful one. I close my eyes and imagine myself hugging my little girl—reminding her she's safe now and *I will never leave her.*

This is how I learn to mother myself.

If Only

WHEN I WAS STILL MARRIED AND PEOPLE WOULD ask how I met my ex, I'd perk up and tell them about our magical "eleven days of love." I'd share the first time we held hands and felt sparks, how I made him jealous with another guy to finally get him to ask me out, and how he got down on one knee to make that first date request.

There were sweet moments, sure. But just like I fabricated a closer bond with my mom to cope with our actual distance, I made up a "meet-cute" about my ex that's about as real as a rom-com. I was so committed to ignoring the red flags that I never tell the full story. Here's the real story:

I'm staying at a co-living "start-up house" for entrepreneurs, set in a three-level Victorian home in San Francisco. I'm smitten with a man I've just met—he's warm, charismatic, and kind, and he asks me so many thoughtful questions. He runs this place alongside an all-male team, and they call their workspace "the war room."

We've made plans to spend time together, and I'm in my room feeling a flutter of anticipation, trying on outfit after outfit until I find the right thing to wear. I brush my teeth, fluff my hair, and take one last look at myself in the mirror before heading downstairs to the café to meet him. I arrive early and take a seat.

Fifteen minutes pass, then thirty, and still no sign of him. I pull out my journal and start writing to pass the time. An hour passes and I begin to worry if he's okay. I walk from room to room, asking if anyone has seen or heard from him. The others don't seem concerned. *He's probably just running late*, they say, which makes me wonder if this kind of behavior is normal for him.

Nearly three hours later, he comes running through the front door with a dead phone and an out-of-breath apology. Without a word, I ask him to join me outside.

"Can I be honest?" I say, standing on the front stoop. He nods. "I don't know if I can trust you."

By the way he sucks in air, caves in his chest, and steps backward, I can tell my words have landed like a punch. He finds his footing and responds quickly. "Trust is the foundation of any relationship," he says. "I'm so sorry I put that into question. I'll make it up to you, I promise. It won't happen again."

There was something about the way he took full ownership and understood the impact of his actions that made me feel safe, like I *could* trust him. But this first argument became our second, third, hundredth, and ultimately, our last. It took me a long time to see the difference between eloquent words and action.

During those "eleven days of love," his business partner asked me if I could coach my ex, because while he had so much potential, his leadership was inconsistent and unreliable. Later, over wine, my ex told me that he wasn't sure if he believed in marriage. In the eleven days I was there, I watched him work relentlessly around the clock and sleep a mere three hours a day, completely ignoring his well-being and health.

Today these are red flags for me. But back then, they felt like a green light.

"It's natural to be drawn to people who feel familiar and like home," my therapist later said. "It's not a coincidence that we date or marry people like our mothers and fathers, because we're trying to heal our childhood wounds by being with someone who feels familiar, yet new. But the problem is, this is not the place we heal our wounds; it's the place we reopen them."

Unconsciously, I saw my relationship with my ex as a chance to "get it right" and have a "do-over." Unlike my mom, he seemed open to change and willing to do the inner work—or at least that was what he told me. He could admit fault and own up to hurtful behavior, which felt like a perfect canvas for me to finally heal my past once and for all. Or so I'd hoped.

When John and I met, I began studying attachment theory with one of his mentors, George Haas, a leader in the field. I wanted to better understand how my early relationships with caregivers had shaped my adult patterns of bonding and relating. I was still trying to crack the code on how I'd spent nine years on relationship autopilot, and more than anything, I wanted to show up for John fully present, with my heart wide open.

One day in class, George says, "One of the core tenets of secure love is that each partner does what they say they'll do. If there's a disconnect between actions and words, distrust and unsafety are introduced to the relationship and before you know it, you're in an insecure dynamic."

I lean forward, on the edge of epiphany. "What if the disconnect between actions and words was my biggest complaint for the entire relationship and yet I continued to stay?" I ask, still trying to make sense of my dynamic with my ex.

"That means you were dealing with abandonment terrors and unprocessed grief from earlier relationships," he says plainly, because this is how George says things. "You prolonged the relationship by telling yourself *If Only*s."

If only . . . I could get him to do what he says he will do.
If only . . . he would take better care of his health.
If only . . . he went to therapy and did the inner work.
If only . . . we could figure out the intimacy piece.
If only . . . he worked less.
If only . . . I could stay focused on what's exciting and good and ignore the rest.
Then . . . everything will be okay, I'll be safe, this relationship will work, and I'll heal the pain of my past.

"You weren't ready to accept what had already happened, what was already lost," he says. "You convinced yourself that you could make things work, but you didn't see him accurately or hold him accountable until the very end, when you left."

The clarity of his words strikes a bell inside my chest. The original *If Only*s appear before me suddenly, and all at once:

If only . . . Mom went to therapy and did the inner work.
If only . . . Mom took care of herself.
If only . . . Mom was capable of meeting me emotionally.
If only . . . Mom addressed her trauma in healthy ways.
If only . . . Mom could see, hear, and attune to me.
Then . . . this ache inside me would finally go away.

It turns out I've been looking for closure and acceptance in all the wrong places. No one else is going to make this ache go away. And maybe I don't need it to go away; maybe I need to let it exist. By letting it exist, I can accept what I lost as a child and finally heal. And I can stop desperately trying to change the past by attempting do-overs in my romantic relationships.

All that's left to address is my own *If Onlys*:

If only . . . I could put down the fantasy that other people will change.
If only . . . I could save myself instead of trying to save others.
If only . . . I could feel my grief rather than run from it.
If only . . . I could set healthy boundaries.
If only . . . I could meet my own emotional needs.
If only . . . I could open myself to real love.
Then . . . I'd realize that I'm okay no matter what.

The real work is not in them.
The real work is in me.
If only . . .

A Safe Place to Land

I'LL ADMIT IT: I'M A RECOVERING FIXAHOLIC WHO gets a high off solving other people's problems. But what I'm realizing is that my urge to solve often comes from my own discomfort. It's far easier to jump into solutions than it is to sit with the raw unease of someone's pain. But that's not love—that's control.

In my next class with George, I ask, "How do I stop trying to fix all the time?"

"Come soothing, not solving," he says. Meaning: stop trying to solve problems that are not your own. Fixing assumes we know best, but soothing creates space for the other person to find their own answers.

George reminds me that people are fully capable of solving their own challenges. But, when we're distressed, the solving part of our brain turns off. Once we help someone feel seen, heard, and understood—once they're emotionally regulated—they'll know what to do. Offering advice or solutions usually backfires because we're not actually seeing the person in the state that they're in. We're not feeling them. We're not sitting with their pain. But everyone has a thing that melts them. A thing that instantly settles their nervous system and brings them back to their center. Our job in relationships is to learn that thing about the other person.

For me, it's getting a cuddle.

For John, it's deeply listening to him so he feels genuinely heard.

The magic of "soothing, not solving" is this: when we stop fixing, we start connecting. Love isn't about answers—it's about being a safe place for someone to land.

Gains

IT'S EASY TO POINT A FINGER AT MY EX AND LIST all my needs he didn't meet. I'm sure he could also point a finger at me and make his own list.

Also: I chose this dynamic; I picked him. And with that in mind, I think a more interesting question to ask is:

What did I *gain* from choosing this dynamic?

In our dynamic, I could hide.

I could dominate and control.

I could avoid true intimacy.

I could talk about vulnerability without experiencing it directly.

I could sidestep resolving the wounds of my past.

I could point to someone as the problem for why I wasn't being brave in my own life.

Filling the Void

THE SUMMER BEFORE MY JUNIOR YEAR OF HIGH school, I got my braces removed, I finally got boobs and curves, and, as my mom put it, I "swanned." Before that, I had a long awkward stage. Boys told me my high forehead made me look like an alien. I had tight curly hair that I tried desperately to straighten so I'd look more like the other girls. My arms were disproportionately long, and my hands were big enough that people pointed them out and laughed. "Don't listen to them—you have piano fingers," my mom would say, trying to reassure me.

On the first day of my junior year, my classmates stared at me as I walked down the hall. This startled me at first. I wondered if I had something on my face or if I had bled through my pants without realizing it. But then one boy tripped over his backpack. Another asked me if I was new around here. And a pack of jocks hollered "Amber got hot" when I walked past them, making me blush. I still felt like the same awkward girl on the inside, but I had tasted power for the first time and I wanted more.

It wouldn't take long for me to discover that the shorter the skirt, the longer the gaze. The tighter the top, the greater the praise. This newfound power happened to coincide with my mom finally leaving my stepdad. While my dad had been entirely absent from my life, leaving me yearning for approval and attention, my stepdad had offered a confusing mix of parental care and creepy behavior. My hunger for male attention was now at an all-time high, while my understanding about why I craved it so much barely kept pace with my developing figure.

My body and appearance became the Thing that would give me love, acceptance, praise, approval, power. The Thing that would resolve my little girl's fear of abandonment and ensure she was safe and worthy of love. By controlling how I looked, I could control how others responded to me. This obsession quickly turned into body dysmorphia and eating disorders, and eventually a full-blown Adderall addiction.

By my freshman year of college, my mom was still locked in a legal battle with my stepdad, who was trying to take her for everything, and it felt like she was losing her mind in the process. She was drinking a lot, talking to herself, and acting more unstable than I'd remembered. It frightened me, and it made me need the Thing even more.

I dropped fifteen pounds I didn't have to lose and began binge drinking my way through the weekend. It felt like the typical college thing to do—a way to numb myself and fit in—but the painful hangovers and my spotty memory of the night only made everything worse. By my sophomore year, I felt starved for love and returned to binge eating to cope. It felt familiar.

I remember my thirteen-year-old self standing in front of the fridge, door open, cool air on my skin. There's a pan of homemade tiramisu inside—my favorite. I'm afraid to eat tiramisu because I've learned that dessert can make me gain weight. But I want it so badly. I look around the house to make sure no one's around. The coast is clear.

I grab a fork and the kitchen timer and set it for fifteen seconds. I walk back to the fridge, open the door, peel the tinfoil off the tiramisu, and begin frantically stuffing my face, pan still on the shelf.

Ding. Time's up. I slowly pull the fork from my mouth, wash it in the sink, and place it inside the dishwasher. I look around again. No witnesses.

While I wasn't new to binge eating, the compulsion became more intense during those college years, when I had more privacy and didn't constantly have to look over my shoulder. I gained all the weight back plus a whole lot more, and it suddenly felt like I'd lost my power. College guys put me in the friend zone. No one hollered when I walked down the street. I thought I had lost the Thing that had made me worthy of love. When I sat next to a classmate who had suddenly become very thin, I asked her what her secret was. "Adderall," she whispered as she wrote down the name of her doctor. "He'll write you a script—no questions."

One week later I got my script and held the Thing that would put me back in control. The Thing that would return me to love, acceptance, and approval. I proved this theory right when I won the heart of a guy who all the girls were after. He picked *me*, so now I must have been worthy. He was emotionally unavailable and avoided intimacy, which I interpreted as mysterious and magnetic. *How interesting* that this is a person I can't decode. *How interesting* that I'm not sure how he feels about me. *How interesting* that he appears super into me one moment and then aloof and distant another. This "magnetism" sent me seesawing between playing it cool and desperately clinging to his every gesture of affection and care. I thought I needed to be perfect, thin, and sexy to be worthy of him—I believed those were the keys to closeness and love.

Adderall became the pill I popped to feel enough.

For a while it seemed to be working, especially when I found myself trying on size-zero jeans at a clothing boutique in my college town. Being this thin brought me a kind of elation that was hard to contain. I stood in front of the mirror, grinning and admiring my flat stomach and the space between my legs; I could almost hear my stepdad's approving comments in my head. Looking like this made me feel powerful and in control, even when one friend whispered to me, "Are you okay? Do you have an eating disorder?" while looking around to make sure no one could hear. "Eating disorder?!" I said, taken aback. "What would give you that idea?"

Technically, at that point, I wasn't lying.

I started with one pill a day, then two, and eventually three or more. I skimmed rock bottom when I had a seizure after an Adderall-infused all-nighter to ace a test, but I didn't fully bottom out until the college boyfriend ghosted me after graduation. After nearly a year of dating, he vanished and was unreachable for weeks, until he finally agreed to meet for coffee. He told me he wanted to be single, but that I was the kind of girl he might one day like to marry. This sent me spinning into stories of panic and not-enoughness, which only fueled my addiction more. But my doctor was now in a different state and could no longer mail the prescriptions. I took one look at an old script, apparently designed using Microsoft Word, and got to work on a forged version.

I already had a relationship with my local pharmacy, so no one ever questioned my script since they had been filling it for nearly a year. But one weekend, when I was heading out of town with friends and fresh out of my fix, I stopped by a new pharmacy feeling agitated and in a rush.

"What's taking so long?" I asked at the counter a few times, nervous and hurried. The pharmacist kept side-eyeing me, which only made my heart pound harder. Just as I was about to leave and give up on the refill, the pharmacist called my name.

Phew, I thought. *I actually pulled this off.*

But then he said, "This prescription isn't real, and I'm on hold with the police right now."

My heart started racing and a movie began playing in my mind at once: the cops arriving, me in handcuffs, a mugshot, a jail cell, the loss of my job, my friends, and everything that mattered to me.

"But this must be your lucky day," the pharmacist said, setting me free with a single sentence. "Your doctor just called back and said there must be some sort of mix-up. He'll handle things from here."

I could tell the pharmacist knew there was no real mix-up, but he had to follow the doctor's orders. I never heard from that doctor again, which didn't surprise me. He'd been handing out prescriptions to college kids like it was candy, and I always suspected he wasn't running his practice by the book.

Still, that moment brought me to my senses. It took me almost losing everything to realize I had already lost myself.

Later, I found a forgotten stash of Adderall in one of my drawers—seventeen pills, to be exact. Or thirty-four if I broke them in half. That gave me thirty-four days to wean myself off and break the addiction. Thirty-four days to let go of a habit that had been spiraling my life into darkness. Some days went surprisingly smoothly; other days I felt like a ravenous animal. But as I slowed my intake, something unexpected happened: I started to feel again. The creative parts of me began to flicker back to life. I found myself more connected to my intuition and what truly mattered to me. I started writing again. I went on long walks. I let myself cry.

During this time, I met a new friend who gave me the book *The Power of Now*, which taught me how to detach from my thoughts. A few months later I followed a hunch and moved to San Francisco—a decision that would ultimately transform my creative life and career. As I filled my days with things that gave me purpose and meaning, my need for outside affirmation began to fade. I no longer wanted to pop a pill to feel like I was enough. And for the first time in my life, I didn't need the Thing to fill the void—I was learning to fill it myself.

Forever

WHEN I TURNED THIRTY, I FINALLY PUT DOWN the story that somewhere out there existed a perfect, un-bloated, gorgeous, voluminously haired, radiant woman who glides through life like a swan. I wanted so badly to be her. But then I met enough powerful, bloated, strong, radiant, I-love-myself-as-I-am kind of women that one day I said, "Fuck you, perfect fantasy swan woman! I'm going to learn to love the real me."

But now I live in LA, where the Perfect Woman crosses my path every seven seconds, haunting me like a ghost. Even though John and I are settling into our relationship, and I'm feeling more secure in our love, I still notice old wounds of not feeling good enough creeping back to the surface.

One evening, in a moment of insecurity and self-sabotage, I start googling photos of John, curious what I might dig up about his past relationships. I know this is an awful idea, but the hungry ghost inside me is the one controlling the mouse. As I scroll through images, getting a window into his art-works, interviews, and older exhibitions, a photo of him and another woman pops out on my screen. *Who the hell is she?*

I wonder, clicking on the photo. *Oh, that's him and one of his very sexy exes—at an art opening.*

As much as I try to keep my mind focused on positive and useful thoughts—"She looks sweet," "Of course he has exes—just like you do," and "They were cute together"—my mind quickly descends into a rabbit hole of comparison and self-doubt.

Against my better judgment, I open up Instagram, search her name, click on her profile, and proceed to scroll through page after page of images. And unlike John, she still has photos of them all over her Instagram. I see them at a marathon (*They ran together?*); in a boat somewhere exotic (*How are her abs so chiseled?*); in front of one of his artworks, looking contemplative (*Don't I have a photo just like this?*).

I scroll back up, browsing through her more recent life (*My life is better*), her new relationship (*My guy is hotter*), and her latest travel (*Her abs aren't so chiseled anymore*) until I'm throwing my phone across the room, sick to my stomach, feeling like an awful, jealous, judgmental version of myself.

What's gotten into me? Why don't I trust this man who's never given me a single reason to question his faithfulness and commitment to our relationship?

→·←

IT'S SPRING BREAK—1997. I'M twelve years old, walking on the beach with my best friend. Up ahead I see my step-dad stretched out on a beach blanket, legs crossed, a tray of shots in hand, laughing. *What is he doing here?* I look around to take in the whole scene: He's surrounded by a group of beautiful young women, college-aged, toned, skinny waists, big breasts, wearing string bikinis. There's a cooler and everyone is drinking out of red cups.

Before I have a chance to slow down and process what's happening, I'm marching toward them full steam. "Excuse me," I say sharply, one hand on my hip. "What are you *doing*?"

He does a double take as a pang of nervousness flashes across his eyes, but his words come out smoothly. "Hey, kiddo," he says. "Oh, I'm just making sure my new friends here have a good time. . . ."

"New friends?" I say, crossing my arms and rolling my eyes. The women look at each other and widen theirs. I can tell I'm making everyone uncomfortable, but I don't care. I stand there for a moment, the silence building, until I cave. "Well, have fun," I say, storming off in search of my mom.

As I walk away, his unmistakable laugh cackles behind me. The girls laugh too. I look back, but he doesn't care. He's still stretched out, legs crossed, having a grand ol' time.

->··<-

THE NIGHT OF THE doomscrolling and ex-stalking, I dream I'm getting out of my car, in a parking lot, in a large city. Manhattan, maybe, but I can't tell. I see John up ahead with his ex. He doesn't know I'm there, so I crouch behind the car, hiding. I feel unsettled, like I'm peering down a well into a life that's no longer mine.

They're smiling and laughing and touching each other's arms. He's looking at her with seductive eyes that say *I want you*. She's biting her lip. She knows exactly how to flirt and express her desire. I feel the urge to run toward them, but I can't. I feel solid like stone, like the life is being drained out of me. I want to look away, but I can't stop staring. It feels like something sharp is digging into my heart.

Then I wake up.

Ouch, I think, touching the tenderness at the center of my chest.

⇥ ⇤

ALL THIS FEAR ABOUT *John leaving me, not being loyal, or another woman taking his attention away from me*, I reflect in my journal, *has nothing to do with John. I'm projecting my unresolved wounds onto him.*

"You were made a part of your parents' drama," Christine adds a few days later. "So you thought you needed to step up, take care of things, and be on the lookout for threats. It's no wonder you're scanning for danger now, anticipating that something might go wrong, waiting for the other shoe to drop. There was a brief moment in your childhood where you got comfortable, thinking, *Oh good, I have a father now, someone I can rely on*, but then seemingly overnight, every-thing shifted. Now that you're comfortable with John, now that you have a partner you can rely on, you're expecting that same familiar and painful shift. If you get too comfortable, it might all fall apart. Just like you're used to."

⇥ ⇤

THAT NIGHT, WHEN JOHN returns home, I tell him about my stalking, my fears, the dream, therapy, and my big realizations. He nods and listens intently as I pace around the living room, putting words to hurts that have long gone unsaid. When I finish, I look at him. I can see on his face

149

that he's heard me, that he understands. He motions for me to come sit with him. I lower into his arms and he kisses my face. I look up and ask the question that's been weighing on my heart:

How do you interact with women in the world? Do you ever feel lust or longing?

"I totally get that question. And honestly, I think it's an important thing for both people in a relationship to know, to feel confident about," he says. "But before I answer, it's really important to me that you know how deeply satisfied I am in that department. If I ever have a desire, or if there's something I want sexually, you can trust that I'll come to you with that, not go outside the relationship. Okay?"

I nod. Hearing the truth in his words, my body softens into him.

"As for how I act with other women ... When I'm in a committed relationship, I'm an extremely loyal person and I'm very mindful of that kind of energy. To be honest, I take a sort of pride in honoring you, and honoring us, when I'm in the world. It makes me feel my integrity, and that's a good feeling for me. And as you know, some of my most meaningful friendships are with women, so it's always super important to me that everyone feels safe and clear and good. I know some people like that sort of unspoken, flirtatious energy— they find it exciting or something. But for me, when I'm in love and committed, that sort of energy just makes me feel uncomfortable and unsafe. It feels cheap and uneasy, and it dishonors everything we have here. Everything I stand for. Does that make sense?"

Hearing his words, I'm settled, and not just because he's very articulate and good with words, but because this time I can feel in my body that his words line up perfectly with his actions. He does as he says—a novel experience for me. I'm learning that I can trust him, who he shows me he is, and that it'll be consistent over time. I *can* relax and be comfortable here—and it won't all blow up.

"Thank you for explaining that," I say. "So you're telling me you might be sticking around for a little while?"

"Forever and forever," he says. "Silly goose."

⇒ ⇐

A FEW WEEKS LATER John and I are lying on the beach in Malibu when a pack of Perfect Women in their itty-bitty bikinis crosses our path. Anxiety courses through me, and my mind starts spiraling. *Is he looking at them? Is he more attracted to them? Should I look more like that? Why is my belly softer? How do they not have cellulite? Does he want them?* As soon as I notice the thoughts, and my elevated heartbeat, I close my eyes, feel the sensation of fear in my chest, and breathe. I remind myself that jumping into a story about how John might not be attracted to me is a *very* old story— and a *very* old pathway in my brain. I remember twelve-year-old me on the beach and I remind her, *You are not your mom. John is not your stepdad. You are safe. You are loved. And you've always been enough.*

My twelve-year-old inhales, my thirty-five-year-old exhales, and I as reach my hand in the air toward John, he takes it without me having to ask.

Conflict

JOHN AND I SHOW UP TO HIS FRIEND'S BIRTHDAY party. A woman appears out of nowhere like a fairy and disappears just as quickly. I recognize her immediately. She's a woman John had a brief fling with a few years back. Supposedly it was pretty racy and adventurous. *Yuck.* John looks at me like *I didn't know she was going to be here* and I look back at him like *This is uncomfortable, but also you've had past lovers and we've talked about this, so what?*

So what? I tell myself as we enter the party, greet the birthday girl, hug old friends and new, and pour ourselves drinks. *So what?* I tell myself when I catch her eyeing me from across the room, looking me up and down with such precision that I can almost hear the voice inside her head saying, *So that's who John ended up with, huh?*

So what? I tell myself when I try to play it cool by starting a conversation with her. But *So what?* is not a game that my body is willing to play anymore.

While my mind is intent on convincing me that this is all very much "no big deal" and "I'm safe here," my body is preparing for battle. It feels as if I'm being transported back in time, thousands of years, and if I don't guard my man, my future offspring are at stake. A kind of primal jealousy boils inside me, and I can't seem to stop it from spilling over.

I excuse myself to the bathroom to recenter. John, who's across the yard chatting with friends, catches my expression as I pass and quickly follows me. Before I reach the door, he catches me, and I say louder than I mean to, "I want to leave, *now*." I'm mortified to have him see me like this, so I slam the door in his face and turn the lock. This doesn't go over so well.

"What's going on with you?" he asks sternly in a tone that sends me straight back into my twelve-year-old body.

"I'm overwhelmed," I say, my voice shaking. "Please leave me alone."

"Why did you slam the door in my face?" he asks sharply, which only intensifies my embarrassment and shame.

"Because I don't want to see you right now," I say. "Please go away."

The rest is a blur. We joust back and forth with our best fighting words—unspoken grievances and frustrations fly until we're in the car flat-out screaming. My inclination to get out of the car and run only makes John's voice get louder, which only escalates my need to flee. It feels like I'm outside my body, floating.

Does this mean we don't belong together?

⇨ ⇦

I'M TWELVE YEARS OLD, and my mom and stepdad have thrown one of their big bashes in the basement of our home. When you descend the stairs to reach this promised land, what you discover is not a normal basement but instead a full bar that looks like something you might find in a downtown hotel. There's a built-in sound system with bass levels I'm always nervous will wake the neighbors. A pool table, foosball, and darts. Not one but three televisions. Lined up inside custom-built maple cabinets are every type of drinking glass you can imagine. My mom and stepdad don't go out to parties; they bring the party home—to their very own sports bar. "Your parents are so cool," my friends tell me. "Is your basement not like this?" I ask.

On this particular night it's late and I should be sleeping, but no one's really keeping tabs on me. I'm filling up a glass of water in the kitchen when I hear raised voices and thumps from the party below. I sneak past Gram, who's watching television in the living room. I open the door to the basement as slowly as I can and tiptoe down the stairs. Before I can even digest the scene in front of me, my heart is racing and I'm sprinting toward my parents. My stepdad's hand is around my mom's throat and she's pressed up against the wall, flailing around like a fish. I pound my fists against his back, screaming, "Stop it! Stop it! Let go of her! Let go of her!" My voice cracks as I scream for him to stop, choking on tears.

"Amber, come here!" Gram yells from the top of the stairs. "Come here right now!" I feel helpless and afraid. I can't leave my mom like this. "Please, stop," I cry out. "Please!"

My stepdad loosens his hand from around my mom's throat, and she wobbles around until she finds her balance. "It's okay, baby," she says, slurring her words.

Gram, now by my side, wraps her arms around me. "Let's go to bed, sweetheart." I walk slowly up each step, looking over my shoulder for any new sign of danger. Gram tucks me in, kisses my forehead, and says, "Don't worry, love, adults fight sometimes." I lie there, frozen, staring at the ceiling, terrified.

This incident is never spoken about again.

→ ⋅ ←

JOHN AND I SIT in silence for a long while in the car and I wonder if this means that we're not a good fit. We're supposed to be in the honeymoon phase of our relationship and we're already screaming at each other? This surely has to be a bad sign—a red flag, right?

As my mind is rehearsing a *Let's just leave it here—we gave it our best shot* speech, John reaches over and grabs my hand, taking me by surprise. "I'm sorry for raising my voice," he says gently, easing a yearning I can't describe in any other way except to say that it freed me.

My mind starts playing a new *Let's keep going—it's your turn to apologize* speech. I take a moment to consider what's mine here. "I'm sorry for slamming the door in your face," I say, turning my head to look into his eyes. "And for not letting you in on what was going on with me."

His body exhales and his breath deepens. "I'm sorry I wasn't able to be more gentle and attuned to you in the way that you needed," he says, pulling me in for a cuddle, speaking words I've never heard, calming the fright of my little girl.

"And I'm sorry I kept trying to push you away and flee," I say, squeezing him tight. He pulls me closer and we just sit there, our bodies coming back into balance with each deep breath.

Oh, I think to myself. *Conflict can be safe. It doesn't have to turn into something threatening or dangerous. It might be uncomfortable, sure, but I don't have to be terrified, and it doesn't mean everything is about to blow up. Maybe conflict means we're willing to go there—to fight to understand and be understood. So long as we mend the ruptures, conflict can actually bring us closer.*

"This is what happens when new couples shack up," Christine confirms a few days later. "You're learning each other and refining the way you take care of each other. I would be more alarmed if this *weren't* happening."

"That's relieving," I say.

"It's natural to see conflict as a threat to the relationship, especially with your history," she says. "But conflict doesn't break up relationships. A lack of repair does."

⇥ ⇤

JOHN AND I GET out of the car and walk back into the party holding hands. Music is playing and our friends are dancing. We look at each other and smile as we move our bodies to the beat. The woman from John's past appears, I smile at her, and I mean it. She smiles back, her body swaying with us to the rhythm.

⇥ ⇤

IN DREAMS, BASEMENTS CAN symbolize dark secrets, what's hidden, the subconscious mind. Reflecting on my own past, I realize how much was happening beneath me. The basement wasn't just a physical space; it was a metaphor for the underlying tensions and hidden conflicts in my family. On the surface, everything seemed perfect—parties, laughter, fun. But beneath that facade lay a darker reality that was unspoken.

For years, I repressed the memory of my stepdad strangling my mom, burying it deep within my subconscious. The trauma didn't disappear; it lodged itself in my body, manifesting as anxiety and unease. I would frequently find myself holding my breath when I panicked or felt threatened, never fully understanding why. But as I reconnect to my past, my gratitude for little Amber deepens. I see how hard she worked to get here, even if it meant leaving parts of herself behind.

As I see my past more clearly, I'm no longer trapped in the cold hospital room with my father or in the dank basement with my stepdad.

Little by little, I liberate myself.

Coiled Cord

I CAN BARELY REMEMBER MY FATHER. I HAVE JUST a few memories of him—talking to him on the phone when I was three years old before his car accident and then seeing him in the hospital after. But what I remember most is my hunger to know him. My longing to be comforted by him. My yearning to feel his attention and delight.

My inventions of him were wide-ranging and generous. He was the voice of every male vocalist on the radio—I would close my eyes and imagine that it was him singing to me. Sometimes he would visit me through the fathers of friends. I'd listen to him offer unsolicited advice with the joy of a dog waiting for her bone. Or he'd crack jokes and I'd laugh with my whole body, even when I didn't fully understand.

I still remember one night, when I was seven years old and at a friend's house for a sleepover. Her dad came in to say good night, sitting on the edge of her bed with a worn-out book in his hands. She snuggled under the covers, her face lighting up as he began to read. I watched from the other bed, feeling a tight knot form in my chest. The way she basked in the warmth of his voice, the way he softened each word just for her—it was like they were in their own little world—a world I longed to be part of. As he kissed her forehead and turned off the light, I thought, *I want a dad who reads to me like that.*

I was twelve years old when I found out my father died. I was in the guest bedroom of my childhood home, wearing a pink tracksuit, playing "work" on the bed. I was pretending I ran a company like my mom, and I answered phones to make sales and communicate with my team. I used a vintage ivory phone with a long coil I wrapped around my fingers.

"This is Amber," I'd say when a call came in. "Yes, we do have that item in stock. Would you like to purchase it?"

My mom walked to the door and I looked up at her. Her face, long and heavy, told me something was wrong. "Baby," she said. "I just got the news that your father died. I'm so sorry."

I held my breath and wrapped the coiled cord around my fingers—tighter and tighter until they turned blue.

⇒ ⇐

I WASN'T SURE HOW I was supposed to feel about the death of a man I could only remember meeting once. The death of a man who took up enormous real estate in my imagination but no actual space in my life. When my father died, I didn't lose the person; I lost the idea of him. But the longing remained.

When my stepdad came into my life, I hoped he'd be the father I'd always wanted, but his unpredictability and volatility only intensified my fear of not being truly loved or accepted. The only other male figure in my life was my granddad, and though he was kind to me, he felt distant and unreachable—an island in the distance with a dim light. Since little me never got her needs met by a loving father, without ever realizing it, I entered every romantic relationship with the same internal question: *Will you be my father?*

Will you take care of me?
Will you make me feel safe?
Will you fill my void of love, closeness, and belonging?
Will you stay and not abandon me?
Will you make me the center of your world?

And when these needs went unmet, because no person is capable of filling needs I haven't yet learned to meet myself, that man and the potential of what our love could be consumed my thoughts but never took root in reality.

My problem was this: I didn't know how to love the person; I only knew how to love the idea of them.

To break this pattern, I had to become the parent I'd never had—the one who would give me the unconditional love and secure attachment I'd been longing for. This meant learning to soothe my own fears, feel the fullness of my emotions, and create the safety and stability that had always felt out of reach.

The solution was this: I would finally learn how to love myself. Cliché, I know, but as it turns out, it's the whole damn thing.

Eight Words

"BRING TO MIND YOUR FIRST MEMORY OF BELIEV-
ing that you needed to be perfect to be loved," Christine says
as I'm stretched out on the couch, my eyes closed. An unfa-
miliar memory appears like a movie being projected onto a
screen.

My father is stomping around the house, gathering his
things. The television is smashed, and remnants of glass are
scattered on the floor of our living room. My mom is crying,
distraught, flailing around, in her own universe. My father
is walking to and from his car, unwilling to make eye contact with me. I stand at the front door, motionless and numb.

"What are you noticing?" Christine asks.

"My dad is getting ready to leave without saying goodbye," I say, through tears. "And I'm frozen. I feel like I've
done something wrong."

"Let your biological dad continue to do his thing without
trying to change him," Christine says. "And now invite your
ideal father figure into the scene to offer you the care and
reassurance you need."

My ideal father bends down next to me. He brushes the
hair away from my eyes and rests his hand on my wet cheek.

161

"I understand that you feel really scared right now," he says gently. "It's okay, I'm here with you." I take a deep breath and my body softens. He pulls me in close, squeezes me tight, and whispers in my ear, "Him leaving has nothing to do with you."

Eight words I've waited my entire life to hear.

Part 3

Be Free

Boundaries

ONE DAY MY MOM AND I ARE TALKING ON THE phone about motherhood. Ever since John and I shared baby names on our first date, I've been imagining what it would feel like to become a mother—both terrified and enlivened by the thought. I tell Mom that I see myself as a vessel and shepherd for the child. The child doesn't belong to me; they are their own person. My responsibility is to nurture, protect, and guide them—to create a safe space for them to explore, become their own person, and thrive. My heart warms as I share this, imagining John and me starting a family one day.

"I did that, right?" my mom says in response to this.

Irritated that she's making my share about herself, and knowing very well that if I answer honestly she'll become defensive and destabilized, I placate her. "You did encourage me to follow my curiosities."

A few weeks later we're on the phone and she's worked up, talking fast, on the verge of tears. "I can't stop thinking about that thing you said about being a mom—are you saying you want me out of your life?"

My shoulders clench and my jaw tightens. I'm tired of our role reversal. I don't want to be the one to soothe her, validate her feelings, and fill her emotional needs. I no longer want to be the parent in this relationship.

"No, Mom," I say. "That had nothing to do with you. I was telling you something that felt meaningful to me about my one day becoming a mother."

"Yeah I know but it feels like you're trying to toss me to the side," she says. "And I did my best, ya know?"

⇒⇐

ONE OF THE SIDE effects of me finding greater meaning—building a life with John, growing close with his family, coming to terms with painful truths about my past—is that my mom has become overwhelmed with fear that she is being "tossed to the side."

It is not lost on me that my ex-stepdad, my ex-husband, and now my mother have all used the same phrase to describe me.

You're tossing me to the side.

Not, *I feel lonely in my life—and I'm looking to you for meaning.*

Not, *You bring up uncomfortable feelings in me and I'm blaming you for them.*

Not, *I have a deep-seated fear of abandonment from my own childhood that is getting triggered by your autonomy and growth.*

But instead—*you* are tossing *me* to the side.

As much as I see the lack of ownership, and know I am not responsible for her feelings, hearing this makes me feel unsettled, uncomfortable, guilty—like I *should* feel bad for having a life separate from her. The grip of guilt runs deep. For too long I have felt an over-responsibility to care for wounds that are not my own.

But this is the discomfort I'm learning to tolerate: someone being disappointed in me or feeling hurt as a result of my choices and living authentically.

"I'm done with this shit," I tell Christine a few days later. "I no longer wish to be the recipient of my mom's unresolved wounds and unprocessed trauma. It's exhausting."

"Good!" Christine says emphatically.

After our call, my mind goes into problem-solving mode until I land on the Thing that will make everything better: I'm going to bring Mom into the therapy room, set clear boundaries, and name my needs.

I make a list:

1. No emotional dumping. I need Mom to find ways to cope with her feelings and unresolved fears in a way that doesn't involve me.
2. No yelling or voice raising.
3. No comments on my body. (Doesn't she know I had an eating disorder for years?!?)
4. I only want to talk one time per week. I don't want to feel pressure or guilt around calling her.
5. No passive-aggressive communication. Find direct ways to communicate feelings and needs.
6. No calling or texting or commenting on social media posts while drinking or under the influence. It's very unsettling for me. (How does she not know this by now?!?)

I want to add two more things to this list—stop drinking, see a therapist—as those feel like the most essential things that would positively impact our relationship, but I'm not sure it's my place to ask for either of them.

Over the next two weeks I write and rewrite my list. I think about how I can speak my needs kindly and respectfully and communicate in a way that she will actually be able to hear. I practice my lines. I walk John through the list several times, asking, "Is it okay for me to ask for that?" I dream about the conversation. And it finally happens, my hands trembling as I enter our Zoom Room.

For the next fifty minutes I share my needs, hoping my mom can hear, understand, and validate me. But aside from apologizing for one specific comment, my mom can't engage with my vulnerability. Instead she explains herself. She rolls her eyes at this whole "therapy thing," reminds us that she's from a different generation (even though she's the same age as Christine), and says "no offense" to Christine but she thinks "we can do this without her." When my eating disorder comes up, she has trouble finding her words. When I express a need or a preference, I notice her irritation and defenses rise.

Normally my not feeling heard or seen would send me spinning into fight, flight, or freeze. But because Christine is present, I feel safe and regulated. And a wild thing happens:

I'm able to see my mom accurately as she is, not as I hope she'll be.

I see the sixty-year-old woman who has an aversion to therapy and doesn't see the point. I see how emotionally stunted and afraid she is, how she never learned healthy communication and coping skills. But mostly I see a little girl who's trapped in some room from her own childhood, a feeling I know all too well.

I think: *I'm still looking to my mom to see me, know me, and meet the needs of my little girl. Here I am, once again, thinking that if I can find the right words, if I can try a little harder, if I can find the Thing that actually works, she will finally get it and this will cure my emotional loneliness and childhood pain. But my mom can't meet me here. She can't even meet herself here. It's time to put this fantasy down and decide who I seek to meet my needs: my mother or myself.*

I decide I'll look to myself, but it's not easy to change a lifetime of conditioning. Days after the boundary conversation, Mom calls me at 9 A.M. in an emotional downpour about some way she's been wronged, and even though I'm stunned at how quickly she seems to ignore the "no emotional dumping" agreement, it will take me another forty-five minutes of listening to and coaching her to finally say, "I have to go." A few days later she'll make a comment about my body, and the words to speak up for myself will remain lodged in my throat. Some weeks after that, when I'm visiting her, she'll spend that time preoccupied in a family drama, unaware of how her behavior and communication style impacts others. At one point I'll play referee between her and my cousin to try to keep the peace. Later, when we're alone, I'll try to reach her, to help her see how she can respond differently, but she'll tell me she feels "picked on." This moment will invite me to learn the lesson that I keep struggling to learn: I cannot change my mother. All I can do is be realistic, adjust my expectations, have compassion for her conditioning, and put the focus back on my own needs and preferences. That's the most loving thing I can do.

Later I'll look back on our therapy session and realize that I didn't set a single boundary. The list I made wasn't a list of boundaries; it was a list of requests, asking her to change her behavior to meet my needs—an impossible goal. So, I'll pull out my journal and make a list of the things I can actually control regardless of my mom's actions—these are the real boundaries:

1. I will screen Mom's calls. If I'm busy and can't talk or simply don't want to, I won't answer. This will make me feel bad and guilty at first, but it's okay to prioritize my well-being.

2. I will not call her or text with her after 5 P.M. so I avoid communicating when she might be under the influence.

3. If she raises her voice, I will exit the conversation or room.

4. I will not take the bait. If Mom says something to get a reaction out of me, I will let it sit there.

5. I will practice detached observation with her—witnessing her behavior without making it personal—so I don't get emotionally hooked.

6. I will let her be in any mess/meltdown/emotional storm she's in, and I will stay in my own energy. I will leave as necessary.

7. I will not try to coach, fix, save, or solve.

8. I will stop looking to Mom for emotional attunement, validation, and mutuality. I will let go of the idea that she will suddenly meet my needs.

9. I will feel the sadness and grief that comes from seeing

her limitations accurately because that is mine and mine alone.

10. As needed, I will communicate boundaries using *I* language around behavior I can control (e.g., "I'm hanging up because you're raising your voice" instead of "Stop yelling," "I have to go" instead of "Stop coming to me for emotional support").

While my mom has expressed her displeasure—"I don't want a relationship built on boundaries"—what I wish she understood is that boundaries aren't a rejection, a distancing tool, or an attempt at pushing away. By setting boundaries, I'm not saying, *Stay away from me.* I'm saying, *I want to have a relationship with you, but in a way that will make me feel safe enough to come closer.*

But living this list is not always simple. And it's definitely not easy. Prioritizing my needs and attuning to my own preferences can leave me feeling anxious, unsettled, and guilty. There are days when I find myself repeating old patterns, but instead of beating myself up, I think:

This is deep work; try again.

I'm finally learning that boundaries aren't about changing others—they're about choosing myself.

I Try to Remember

FOR A LONG TIME I TRIED TO GET THE PEOPLE who hurt and disappointed me to *get it*. A hopeful part of me thought that if I could find the "right words," they'd finally understand. They'd acknowledge how their behavior impacted and harmed me, they'd validate my pain, and they'd apologize. Like *really* apologize. Not that "I'm sorry you're upset" kind of bullshit. I wanted something honest and heartfelt. Something that showed self-reflection and genuine remorse. I believed that once I received this, I would finally be free. But that was just another trap. Healing didn't come from getting them to understand—it came from letting go of needing them to.

I try to remember: The only one who needs to *get it* is me.

And Also

ON SOME LEVEL, EVEN AFTER ALL THIS WORK and learning, I also realize that I'm writing this very book in hopes that my mom will read it and, one day, possibly change.

The hopeful part of me will always be there. Art, like love, is a hopeful thing.

The Land

FOR SIX MONTHS MY EX AND I WENT BACK AND forth on what to do with the land we shared. My initial shame and guilt at having left my husband for another man prevented me from believing I deserved any part of it. Even though I had found the plot of land and it was our only shared asset—having nearly doubled in value in the year since we bought it—I still believed, on some level, that I should be punished for my "bad behavior." After all, there was no way I could have my cake and eat it too. Logically, I knew that how I left the relationship had nothing to do with our shared rights to the land, but the grip of shame was too strong.

With friends in one ear reminding me not to be taken advantage of and my ex-husband in the other ear telling me why he was entitled to the land, I felt like a Ping-Pong ball with no place to land. Googling "how do I peacefully resolve divorce conflicts?" at two in the morning didn't help either. Eventually I realized I was looking to everyone but myself for answers.

I get out of my car at Topanga State Park and begin walking

up my favorite trail. I find that moving my body in nature helps me listen.

What do I want? I ask myself as I climb steps of natural stone, working up a sweat.

I want to keep the past in the past and start fresh with John.

What else do I want? I ask as I reach a vista of rolling hills.

I want to let go of the land, but I'm not giving it up for free.

What else do I want? I ask as I follow a narrow path down to a creek. The answer to this one comes more slowly, but by the end of the hike, I'm clear:

I want to be bought out, but I don't need half. I just want to be made whole.

Reaching this conclusion, I realize the part of me that longs for harmony and peace is very much alive. And also, some fights just aren't worth it—especially when the cost is my peace of mind. I get back in the car and FaceTime my mom, who's skilled at business negotiations.

"Hey, baby."

"Hey, Mom, I need your help," I say.

"Talk to me," she says.

I explain that I'm struggling to get to a resolution around the land and how I feel like we need an outside mediator to negotiate a fair buyout.

"I'm your girl," she says. "I'll call him this afternoon."

Two days later she has news. "Your ex is sending your first payment today with two more installments coming."

"That was fast!" I say, months of pressure falling instantly off my shoulders. "What did you say?"

"I told him that we have a firm buyout number and there's

no negotiation. Otherwise, we can put the land on the market and split the proceeds, which is a whole lot more than what we're asking for. He agreed very quickly."

Although my mom is a natural dealmaker who taught me how to be a businesswoman, she never ceases to amaze me when I get a front-row seat to her genius.

"Thanks, Mom, I really appreciate your help."

"I'm always just a phone call away," she says, and I can almost see her satisfied smile.

It Was Always Leading Here

IT WASN'T *ALL* TUMULTUOUS, WITH MY EX AND me. Alongside the roller coaster of divorce proceedings, land negotiations, angry outbursts, and finger-pointing, there were beautiful moments of kindness, honesty, and peace.

"It's not only you who left," he admits to me on one of our last calls. "I'd been resisting you for a long time, and I'd been resisting my own potential. I was at war with my self-worth and value, and I never felt rooted or whole."

His words are a salve. "You have no idea how much it means to hear you say that." My voice cracks as tears come. "I'm so sorry I hurt you."

"Thank you," he says softly. "And I understand. What else were you going to do?"

"I mean . . . someone had to pull the plug," I say, both of us laughing.

"Please tell John that I'm deeply grateful to him and hold nothing against him," he adds. "He was a very powerful and confronting mirror for me, but I also felt a deep bond with him and his presence was a gift."

As we go back and forth, each taking responsibility for our part, a calmness and a peace enter the dynamic. My heart reopens. I find myself overwhelmed by remembering that my ex is a kind, warm, and generous person; he just wasn't *my* person.

A few days later I sit down at my desk, open my laptop, and google "get divorced quickly." I learn that an "uncontested divorce" is a fancy way of saying, "We can dissolve your marriage in ninety days or less—all online—if you and your ex are on the same page."

Thankfully, we are now. In our nine years together, we never once shared a bank account. We never owned a home, 401Ks, or stocks. I didn't take his last name, nor he mine. Now that the land is settled, we're in agreement that what's fair is for me to keep what's mine and for him to keep what's his— and for us to make this process as pain-free as possible.

I click a button that says "Get divorced," enter some basic information, add "Expedited divorce" to my cart for $2,247, check a box that says "My spouse is willing to cooperate," and check out. Moments later I receive a receipt and email notification letting me know the divorce is in motion. I forward it to my ex so he can Venmo me half the bill. I look at the date on my computer. It's October 27. I grab my phone to text him.

Our divorce is underway. I also just realized it's October 27. Our first date was nine years ago today. Nine in numerology and tarot symbolizes completion. It means that a full cycle is complete and all lessons from the previous years have been learned. How auspicious! I wanted to take a moment to celebrate you and what we shared. I'm very grateful for the lessons, adventures, and memories we created together—and who we became in the container of our love. I genuinely wish nothing but goodness for you in what comes next, and I will always cheer for you and your happiness.

Moments later he responds, *Happy nine years. I am truly proud of both of us. My love is as alive as it was nine years ago, but now it's evolved into something different. I'm wishing for your happiness always.*

⇒·⇐

MONTHS LATER I OPEN Facebook and see a photo on my newsfeed: two hands clasping, each with a matching tattoo. I look closer, curious whose hands I'm looking at. *Oh! This is my ex and another woman!*

I click over to her profile and am smitten to see her describe my ex as her "forever love." The depth of my joy and relief is hard to explain. It feels akin to how a sister might feel when her brother meets their person. This person, who I spent more than a quarter of my life with, is *in love.* I'm giddy like a schoolgirl, hopeful it works out. I pop over to her Instagram and see videos of them building a life on the land that was once ours. My ego gets involved for a moment—that was *my* land—but I laugh at myself and brush it off. I'm genuinely happy that they are taking care of the land and building a beautiful life there.

I'm so happy for you, I message him.

Over the coming months and years, I'll come to learn through social media that he has gotten engaged and later married. Even though we've lost touch in many ways, I feel grateful for these small glimpses into his life. I can't help but think about our path together, and how it was always leading here.

Pulling the plug didn't just send *me* on a journey of transformation, healing, and awakening—it did the same for him too.

My friend Erin was right: liberation is a two-way street.

Brooklyn Trash

"I KNOW YOU'RE SENTIMENTAL, MOM," I SAY. "BUT I need you to follow my lead this weekend. I don't want to take a bunch of stuff from my past with me to LA."

"It's your stuff!" she says, raising her hands in the air. But I'm skeptical—she always has a way of clinging to my history as if it were her own. I open the door to my old loft in Brooklyn, the place my ex and I lived together before we left for Todos Santos, and my mom gasps.

"Nothing has changed," she says.

"It does look the same," I say.

My eyes scan the room. My art still lines the walls, the grand piano stands where it always stood, and my journals and books line the walls. This apartment has been in my ex's family for well over a decade, and we're here to clear out my belongings so he can figure out what to do with the place.

"Is it weird for you to be here?" she asks.

"No, actually," I say. "I feel neutral."

Mom nods but doesn't say anything. I get the sense that it's weird for *her* to be here.

"All right, let's get moving," I say, jumping into gear, separating all of my things into three piles:

Keep.

Goodwill.

Trash.

I walk over to a stack of journals and start tossing them into an oversize trash bag.

"You're throwing away your journals?" Mom asks with a look of concern.

"I kept a couple," I say. "I don't need all the thoughts of my past to come with me. I feel complete."

I open a box of old photographs from college and quickly flip through them. My heart aches for the girl back then who thought she needed to be pretty, perfect, and thin to be worthy of love. I empty the box of photos into the trash.

"You're not keeping any of those, either?"

"I put a few keepers to the side," I say, smiling.

By the end of the day, we manage to sift through most of my things. We have twenty bags of trash, five boxes for Goodwill, and a carry-on suitcase worth of stuff that I'm taking with me. I place the bags of trash in the elevator, head to the ground floor, and toss them out one by one into the dumpster.

Mom waves from across the street as she blows out a cloud of smoke.

"Ready for a celebratory dinner?" I yell out.

"Let's do it!" she says, with a skip in her step.

A few hours later, when we're leaving dinner and getting into our Uber, I look at my phone. Eleven missed calls. *That's strange*, I think. My phone starts to ring from a number I don't recognize.

"Hello," I say.

"Oh, hello, is this Amber?" a woman with an Australian accent says on the other end of the line.

"Yes, it is," I say.

"Are you okay?" she asks.

My mom glances over with worried eyes.

"I am, yes," I say. "Why do you ask?"

"A small group of people are really worried for your life right now," she says. "Hundreds of your journals, photographs, book flyers, and business cards are spread out across the streets of Brooklyn."

"Oh no," I say. "I did toss them out in the trash earlier today."

"Amber," Mom says, her brain kicking into overdrive. "This is bad, really bad. What if someone steals your identity? What if they find out private things about you? I told you we should have shredded those. This isn't the last we're going to hear about this. . . ."

"This is kind of hilarious," I say, raising my hands to slow her down. "Everything is okay, Mom."

We arrive at the address and, sure enough, my things are spread across both sides of the street, photographs blowing in the wind, journals strewn about and open face up, others stacked in neat piles. I take in the scene, Mom's expression of panicked horror, and I can't help but laugh.

"This isn't funny," Mom says, lighting a cigarette with one hand as she lunges for a photo of me with the other. "Why are you laughing?"

"I don't know exactly . . . it seems ironic. My relationship with my ex was so public and curated, and the truth of how I really felt was always kept hidden. And now, when I finally stop caring about all that, my most tightly held secrets end up all over the streets of Brooklyn for anyone to see. It seems kind of fitting."

"Well, if this gets out, it's not going to look good. We need a story, and this is what I think our story should be: when we were taking the trash down the elevator to shred and dispose of properly, someone stole a few of the bags. . . ."

"Mom, Mom . . ." I say, tilting my head back as I laugh. "It's okay. Really. I don't care what people think about this. And *no one* is going to care. Even if they did for some bizarre reason, I don't care if people look at the journals and read my innermost thoughts. I don't need to craft some narrative about my life anymore. Really, it's okay."

"Okay . . ." she says, taking a drag. "It's *your* stuff."

My mom acknowledging that I have my own stuff—metaphorically as well as physically—that she doesn't need to involve herself in is a small miracle. And me being okay with our difference of opinion on how to handle this is an even more important one. Her stuff and my stuff have long been intertwined in unhealthy ways. I stepped in to help her navigate "her stuff" way too young and she overstepped into "my stuff" for way too long.

I get to choose what I do with *my stuff.* I don't need a story. I don't need my mom's approval.

Some might call that free.

Nails

I'M AT A NAIL SALON IN LOS ANGELES GETTING A manicure. A woman—blond, rail thin, tall, stylish—walks in with her preteen daughter and they sit side by side to get pedicures. For the next forty-five minutes this mother talks with the owner of the salon about all of her aging and beauty "hacks."

"I'm hungry when I wake up, but if I have water with lemon, I find that my hunger goes away.

"I used to get Botox and fillers with so-and-so, but now I use so-and-so—it looks more natural.

"I sip slowly on bone broth all day to stay full. That took me from a size two to a size zero.

"I don't do extremes, though. I allow myself to have sugar once a month."

Every once in a while her daughter looks up from her iPhone and glances at her mom, who doesn't seem to notice. I wonder what the girl is thinking. I wonder how hearing this makes her feel. I wonder how it will impact her sense of self and who she thinks she'll need to become to be worthy of love.

It takes every ounce of me to not grab hold of her and say:

Your mom learned a long time ago that she needed to be beautiful and perfect to be loved and to feel safe in this world. But love isn't earned through perfection—it's found by embracing your messy, imperfect, authentic self.

I'm not sure that would go over well, so I look to my right and imagine my twelve-year-old self sitting in the chair next to me. She smiles, self-conscious and unsure. I tell her this:

I learned a long time ago that I needed to be beautiful and perfect to be loved and to feel safe in this world. But love isn't earned through perfection—it's found by embracing your messy, imperfect, authentic self.

My twelve-year-old self looks up at me, holds eye contact, and smiles, this time more sure.

"Is this what healing looks like?" she asks.

This is what healing looks like.

We Heal in All Directions

"WHEN YOU WERE A KID AND TURNED DOWN THE music at our parties so you could sleep, I bet that was really hard," my mom says.

What has she been reading? I think but do not say aloud. "Yeah, it was hard. Thank you for acknowledging that."

"I'm sorry. I'm so, so sorry."

"I appreciate the apology, Mom, but there's more to it. What I always longed for was for you to put yourself in my shoes and consider my experience. Because what your actions showed me was that you were more interested in partying with your friends than making sure I was okay and well. And so it became my job to take care of myself."

Normally I wouldn't say this to my mom—I rarely think she can handle my truth. But I'm learning to speak honestly without needing to manage her reaction. I'm speaking up to honor my experience, to break the habit of swallowing it, but not to change her.

"That's not true; I *did* prioritize you," she says quickly, out of habit, and then begins listing all the ways in which she did. *Here we go again*, I think. But I sit there, nodding, trying my damnedest not to take the bait.

Eventually she stops, and for a brief moment she slows down and takes me in. "That must have been really hard."

I let her acknowledgment land. "It was hard," I say, and her face scrunches.

You heal in all directions, I think.

>-<

"I'M SO GLAD YOU'RE happy, Amber," Gram calls to tell me. "What you did took a lot of guts."

"Thanks, Gram," I say, her words wrapping around me like a hug. "I've felt so alone at times in this transition—like no one really understood—so it means more than you know to hear you say that."

"You also made me think about my own life," she adds. "I should have left your granddad much sooner than I did, but I was a housewife in the sixties. I knew he was up to no good, having affairs and being dishonest. But what was I supposed to do? I didn't have a job, I couldn't buy a house, I had two girls to raise. I stayed because I didn't think I had another choice, so I put up with behavior that wasn't okay. I'll always have fondness for your ex because he was a nice man, but I'm glad you're doing what's right for you. It's so brave, my love. I'm very proud of you."

You heal in all directions.

>-<

I'M AT AN EVENT for my book in Chicago, talking about facing our fears and creating a healthy relationship with our

188

emotions. "Our feelings aren't the problem," I say. "It's our relationship to them. Growing up, I learned to feel my positive emotions and repress the so-called negative ones, but that only created more suffering and pain." My granddad is sitting in the front row, nodding, a surprise to me.

When I was a kid, my granddad was a gregarious but distant figure, known to be "tough." My mom told me stories of being whipped with the branches of a weeping willow when she'd been "bad" as a girl, and how after she discovered his affair and went after his mistress, she received a beating. But she also said that he was a very loving father who "had her back" and helped her start her first business. These inconsistencies in her stories of him helped me make sense of my mom's trauma and have compassion for her past, but they also made me feel afraid of my granddad. We'd never once had an intimate conversation.

But now, as he sits in the front row, I see a stoic smile through his tough exterior. I'm worried he might think this whole topic is a sham, but I get some sense that he might be enjoying himself. When I say my final words, he's the first in the audience to his feet, emphatically clapping louder than everyone, a beaming smile on his face.

Afterward we get dinner, and even before we sit down, he's telling me about his fears, his feelings, and what keeps him up at night. He's sharing so openly and generously that it makes me wonder if anyone has ever asked him, "How are you *really* feeling?" That night, for the first time, I see my granddad. I get to know him more deeply. He lets me in. By being honest about my own feelings, it seems I've given him permission to do the same.

You heal in all directions, I think.

→·←

MY MOM AND I are sitting at a table next to the sea, the sky painted blush and apricot. She is not smoking a cigarette because, after forty-five years, she has quit.

"If you could go back and change anything about your relationships with men, would you?" I ask.

"Hmm," she says, sitting taller. She thinks and then says, "I would trust them more." I'm inclined to probe, but I let her words sit there for a moment instead.

"Or wait, that's not it," she says. "I would trust *me* more. I would trust my judgment better. And I'd expect that I deserve more instead of just settling. When I got my ass kicked by a man, I thought I deserved it. I didn't deserve that."

"No, Mom, you did *not* deserve that."

Later that night my mom surprises me when she says, "I know parts of your childhood were fucked up and I didn't know how to deal with things right." Her voice is cracking; tears are sliding down her face. "I lost your dad. I was doing my best to give you a good life. I know, I know, I'm not supposed to say I was 'doing my best,' but really I was. Of course there was chaos. I was a fucked-up twenty-two-year-old who didn't know what the hell she was doing. It was hard, but you were my little miracle. I wouldn't be who I am today without you."

By this point, we're both crying, and it dawns on me that my mom is right. I hadn't really considered her part of the story. Maybe because I've been so angry at her. Maybe because it's hard for children to do that sometimes. And also, until now, she never let me in on what her experience was like.

By letting me see her, by letting me feel her pain, she

unlocks a key to the cage around my heart. I let her in, I let her come closer. Compassion floods me.

"I'll be honest," she says. "There are a few old memories I'm surprised you haven't brought up yet."

"Oh yeah?" I say. "Which ones?"

"Oh, I'm not giving you any more ammunition."

And we laugh.

We heal in all directions, I think.

It's Both

IT'S EASY TO LOOK AT MY PAST AND POINT A finger at my parents:

You were irresponsible.
You were selfish.
You were inconsiderate.
You were unpredictable.
You caused me tremendous pain and never took responsibility.

But also:

You were colorful.
You had a layered past.
You were ambitious and entrepreneurial.
You pushed edges and challenged norms and created beauty.
You encouraged the same in me.

I carry the wounds, but I also carry the gifts—it's both. And now, I'm left to weave them together into something whole.

Baskets

AN OLD PROVERB SAYS THAT WHEN WE COME into this life, our parents hand us two baskets: one full of burdens, and another full of blessings. It is our task to lighten our basket of burdens and add to our basket of blessings. At the end of our lives, we hand down our own baskets to the next generation.

Why are you writing this book? people often ask me.

Because I need to, I say.

The real answer is this: I'm writing this book for me—so I can heal. So I can lighten my basket of burdens by making sense of my history. So I can, hopefully, pass on more blessings to my children.

Tell the Truth

THE YEAR AFTER I LEAVE MY MARRIAGE, I'M ON A podcast tour, promoting my second book, *The Answers Are Within You*. This is a book I wrote when I was with my ex, feeling totally alone in our relationship. It's also a book that I only now realize I wrote as an invitation to myself. *Have the courage to listen to and trust yourself*, I wrote on the back cover. Oh, how much I needed to heed my own advice. Creativity can be a trickster that way—we create what we need most.

Podcast after podcast, I find myself tongue-tied, disconnected, and not in my usual flow. Interviews generally come naturally to me because of my one rule: I tell the truth about my life.

But I'm not telling the truth in these interviews—I'm hiding it. While my readers and online community know my ex and I have separated, they do not know I have fallen in love with John. They don't even know I'm in a new relationship.

There's a good reason for this: as someone who's been living their life out loud on the internet for well over a decade, I wanted to savor and be present in our love story without the opinions, judgments, and big feelings of others, which

I've already gotten plenty of. But that admission also points to a deeper truth: I'm afraid of what people will think. I'm nervous that if I tell the truth about my life, I'll be judged.

In interview after interview, I keep my private and public selves separate. I spout out wisdom about how rejection is a blessing, why we must let go of what people think, and the importance of living with integrity and authenticity, but I do not model this. At the end of each interview, I crumple to the floor with relief that it's over, sick over how uncomfortable it all felt.

I realize that without noticing, I went right back to doing the Thing I do: I'm adjusting myself to fit the expectations of others. "The Good Girl Harmony Myth," my friend Majo calls it. "It's the tendency to seek and keep harmony instead of embracing the conflict and confrontation needed for your growth."

I no longer wish to be this woman. The one who alters herself to please others. The one who hides her truth and holds back her voice out of fear of how others will respond. I want to be a woman who lives for herself. Who honors her truth proudly. Who has the courage to listen to and trust herself and know who the fuck she is.

"The good girl reclaims her power when she shares her voice and truth," Majo says. And so I decide it's time to share our love story with the world.

→ ←

FORTY DRAFTS LATER I read my post aloud to John, Christine, my agent, and a few close friends. They smile and nod and agree that it's time. John and I select a few photos together, and then I share it, heart racing, before quickly walking away from my phone.

I've been trying to find the "right" words to share what I'm about to share with you, and I've finally come to realize that there are no right words. There are only true ones.

Here's what's true for me right now: I've been experiencing the most extraordinary love I've ever known. A kind of love so present, so honest, and so healing that simply thinking about it makes my eyes well with tears.

As someone who's made a career of sharing my truth, it's been refreshing to keep this love sacred and close to my chest. I've been immersed in living our story rather than sharing it. It's been wildly liberating.

And if I'm totally honest, part of my hesitation to share has been to protect the hearts of people from my past and to avoid the potential backlash of people saying I've "moved on too quickly." I've also been reckoning with the shame of being a "bad girl" for ending my marriage alongside the guilt of being the happiest I've ever been.

So why am I sharing now?

My therapist and I have been diving into the origins of what she calls the "pleasing disease." We've been exploring my history of self-betrayal—all the ways I learned to abandon myself to keep the harmony and peace. It's funny because I thought I was so good at living in accordance with my truth, but I'm realizing that hasn't always been the case.

Well, I'm learning to say "fuck it" to that. To the performing. The perfecting. The peacemaking. The smile and nod like everything is okay when my insides are crawling. The over-concern with what people think of me.

My life is now calling for greater levels of authenticity, integrity, and freedom. It's calling for me to put down the old story that I'm responsible for other people's emotions— and instead to live from unshakable truth.

My truth is this: I love John with every ounce of my being. Meeting him opened a door to my heart that I didn't know could be unlocked. He astounds me with his presence, his integrity, his sensitivity, his vision and creativity and care—the way he moves through the world without pretenses or pretending. And my god, do I feel loved by him. So loved. Loving him and being loved by him is the greatest joy I've ever known.

My agent calls me a few hours later. "Did you see?"

"See what?"

"The responses you're getting."

"Oh god, is it bad?"

"No—it's beautiful."

You literally expressed exactly what I'm feeling.

I went through something very similar.

It's like you were writing from my own heart.

Thank you for putting into words what I've experienced but never really had the words to explain.

I'm overwhelmed by all of the positive comments, the private messages, the emails I'm receiving—and surprised by how much my experience is resonating with others. Thousands of kind and encouraging messages pour in. And one I don't expect: an email from my ex-stepdad.

Life throws out a lot of curves. . . . Sad to read about your divorce . . . Sorry, I have not read your books or followed you. Brings up too much pain and sadness . . . This is my attempt to reach out.

His words crawl into my throat and suck out the air. I look at my email list to see how he learned this news . . . only to realize he's been reading every single email I've written over the years, which makes me shudder.

I immediately call Gram, shaking.

"Block him," she says definitively.

"Is that okay? Am I allowed to do that?" I wonder, noticing that old story creeping back in—that I left and hurt him, and "It's never too late to say you're sorry."

"Amber, this has nothing to do with you. He was an adult man and you were a child. He's trying to manipulate you. You owe him nothing. Block him."

She's right. And I do. I block him, reminding myself of the abusive dynamic my friend Vienna pointed out and how it's not my duty to take care of his emotional needs. That's a lesson I keep relearning and a boundary I need to hold.

Thank you, Gram.

My life, my truth, my voice—no more apologies.

"I'll Always Come Back"

JOHN AND I ARE IN VIENNA, HAVING DRINKS AT AN outside café with a group of friends. At one point, John gets up from the table, strolls over to the nearby fence lined with lush greenery, opens a hidden door, and peers inside. He looks back at the group, smiles, and slips through the frame. A few moments later, his friend Megan gets up from the table and follows after him.

The soft thumping of feet, the creaking of swings, and the gleeful laughter of two adults playing in a playground like kids creates a pang of jealousy inside me. I take a sip of wine and contemplate my next move. I can wallow in the story that I wasn't invited or I can invite myself in.

I leave the table and slip through the door, discovering the playground of my childhood dreams. I stand in awe, marveling at the intricate woodwork, the graceful curves of the metallic slides, the orderly rows of swings, and the canopy of towering trees. Simply, Vienna is different. I spot a large, netted, circular tire swing in the distance and run toward it like I'm back in my eight-year-old body. I fall back into the

Amber Rae

swing's embrace and look up to find a sea of stars above me. A grin spreads across my face—childlike, wistful. I think of little me, spinning stories about her father in a playground just like this—grasping for a love that always felt just out of reach.

John walks over and says, "I've got you," as he begins to gently push me. I close my eyes, the crisp air caressing my skin, the scent of mulch taking me back to my roots. "I love you, Amber Rae," he says.

"I love you, John Messinger," I say back. After a few minutes of swinging, I realize that John is no longer behind me. He must have ventured off at some point. I start to wonder when he left, and as my swing starts to slow, if he'll return. But just like that, before the swing starts to lose momentum, he returns, pushes me skyward, keeping my rhythm in time.

"Where did you go?" I ask, glancing back at him.

"I may leave for a little while sometimes," he says with a gentle push. "But I'll always come back to you."

Seven words my little girl has never known.

Baggage

"WHAT'S IT LIKE BEING WITH AMBER WHILE SHE'S confronting and resolving so much of her past?" my friend Melissa asks John during a visit. I perk up, intrigued by the question. John looks at her thoughtfully before he responds. I can tell he wants to be sensitive to my feelings, but also, he wants to say what he means. Eventually, he describes it like this: It's as if she took all the baggage from her life and spread it out across the living room floor. She opened each suitcase, inspected each item inside, and asked:

1. Where did this come from?
2. Is this helping me or hurting me?
3. Do I want to keep this or let it go?

John, with his knack for metaphors, perfectly captures my healing process. Just like I went through all the physical remnants of my past in my Brooklyn apartment, I'm now carefully examining each piece of emotional baggage and making deliberate choices:

This old bag of stories about my lovability and worthiness? Toss it out. *I will never leave me.*

My easygoingness? Keep it, but not at the expense of sacrificing my needs. *My needs are worthy of being met.*

The tendency to feel guilty or "bad" when I do what's right for me? Discard it. *Disappointing others is a skill.*

My creative and entrepreneurial spirit? I'll keep that, but not when work becomes a form of avoidance. *Rest is productive.*

Later I asked him, "How did my going through this process feel for you? Was it a lot?"

"I wouldn't say *a lot*," he said. "Was it challenging at times? Sure, a bit. It's not always easy seeing someone you love going through so much, but also, it wasn't a lot for me because you never made it mine to carry."

He's right: I'm the one I was looking for.

Tolls

ONE DAY JOHN COMES HOME FROM WORK FLUS-
tered and frustrated. The studio assistant he hired is not the
right fit, and after many feedback conversations and attempts
to make the relationship work, he still isn't pleased with the
work she's doing.

"What's worse, I feel like I'm walking on eggshells, because every time I go to show her what I *do* want, she re-
treats or gets defensive. She even admitted that it's hard for
her to receive feedback and not take it personally. Now I
find myself dreading going to the studio."

"Do you think it's time to let her go?" I ask.

"But I spent so much time training her, and to have to hire
and train someone new right now just feels like such a waste
of energy. Maybe I can find a way to make this work. . . ."

As John shares, I can't help but smile, feeling the depth of
this desire to "make it work"—even when all the signs say it
isn't. It's a familiar pattern—the effort to salvage something
that might not be salvageable, clinging to the hope that trying harder will change things. John's presence helped me become aware of this pattern with my ex, and it's meaningful

that I now get to support him in remembering to prioritize his needs too.

"The real cost I see here is the toll this is taking on your well-being, creativity, and peace of mind," I say. "I understand how much of a hassle it will be starting again with a new assistant, but if you're dreading going to your studio to make art, the very thing you love so deeply—*that's* a waste of energy. Something I've noticed about you is that when you're a maybe, you're a no. Doubt for you usually means don't."

By the way John pauses and takes in my words, I can tell he's listening closely. It's not long before he releases his assistant—and himself—and finds a more aligned fit. This is the delicate balance between holding on and letting go. Sometimes, preserving your own peace is the most important investment of all.

John and I will always have work to do on ourselves, but our love is a safe place to address our blind spots, triggers, and wounds. I once believed I had to be fully healed to be ready and available for love. But as my friend Vienna says, "Since it is relationships that wound us, it must be through relationships that we heal."

The Egg

JOHN AND I STROLL ALONGSIDE THE CREEK BEHIND our home, the gentle rustle of leaves accompanying the symphony of birds and the babble of the creek. Hand in hand, we hop from rock to rock across the water, the tail of my blue floral dress—the one I was wearing the day we met—draped around my arm. Our path leads to a boulder, where sun splashes through the lush canopy of trees.

"Want to meditate here?" he asks.

"Sounds perfect."

We sit down and lift our faces toward the sun. John sets a timer on his phone for twenty minutes. I close my eyes and listen to the chorus of nature, a gentle smile spreading across my lips. When the timer sounds, I open my eyes slowly, feeling the buzz of the present moment.

"I have something for you," he says, sweeping the hair away from my face, kissing my shoulder. He pulls an intricately hand-carved wooden egg from his pocket, the wood aged with time. He holds the egg in his palm, and tells me how the egg is a symbol of creation and eternity.

"There's an ancient unspoken knowing between us," he says. "It's always been there, it always will be. It's like some language we learned long ago. And as someone who's always been good at finding the right words, I find that in the face of us, there are no words for this."

He hands me the egg. The wooden treasure is smooth to the touch. "Open it," he says. I glance down to unscrew it, and when I look up, John is bending down on one knee.

My heart swells, and my pulse quickens. I open the egg, revealing a ring—sparkly, delicate, adorned with intricate botanical carvings—designed by him for me. I raise my gaze to meet him, cheeks wet with tears. His eyes are bright and knowing, inviting and infinite. I find myself lost in them now just like the moment we met.

"Will you marry me?" he says.

"Yes!" I say, leaping into his embrace. "I've never been more sure of anything ever."

The Dress

"WE'RE GETTING MARRIED IN TWO WEEKS AND I still don't have a dress," I say to John over a game of rummikub in our backyard, drinking sparkling water out of wineglasses.

I show him my options. One's too country-looking. One's too fancy. One just doesn't feel like me. This is a simple wedding—we put it together in a week, we're hosting it in our backyard, and it's only for our immediate family.

"Give me your phone," John says, reaching his hand out. I look at him and smirk, thinking about the fact that I've seen him on his computer approximately twelve times since we've met. "What? You think I don't know how to do internet things?" he says. "I'm actually good at keyword searches. It's my one true skill on this thing."

"Oh really?" I say, grinning, handing over my phone.

"White country dress," he says slowly while typing it into Google with one finger, just like Gram. He swipes his finger for a few minutes and then taps. "Here," he says, handing the phone back to me. "I found it."

It's an A-line ankle-length dress fitted around the waist, with an all-over floral eyelet design. The slender straps, square neckline, and hemline are all trimmed with petite ruffles. And it's made from organic cotton.

"This dress is perfect," I say. "It feels exactly like me."

"I know," he says, smiling. "Don't act so surprised."

It's moments like this that remind me of the ease I feel at being known and seen so deeply by John—from the fabric of my ideal dress to the fabric of my being.

Glass Doors

ON A SUNNY FRIDAY IN NOVEMBER, I MARRIED
the love of my life under a cottonwood tree in our backyard.
Nine guests were present, three of whom were under the
age of twelve. There was no pitch to *Vogue*. No ridiculously
expensive custom-made dress. No florist, no live music, and
certainly no camels. Much to my dismay, there was also no
photographer—a fact I still give John a hard time about today. But it was, in every sense of the word, perfect. Perfect
not because it looked good on the surface, but because it felt
real from within.

I stood in front of two glass doors—another passageway, this time into the life I created by design, not default. I
walked down the aisle certain, thinking, *This is who I get to
be with for the rest of my life.* When the ceremony began, our
family *ooh*ed and *ahh*ed as a belly laugh erupted through me,
my head tilting back. But this time there was no pretending.
The laughter came from somewhere deep, unforced, true—I
was relieved to now know the difference.

The moment came when it was time for us to share the
vows we wrote together:

Amber Rae

*I vow to remind you each day that you are the most
      lovable person I've ever known.*
*I vow to encourage you to be the brightest and most
      authentic version of yourself.*
*I vow to fully listen to you so you feel seen and heard
      and understood.*
*I vow to be present and attuned to you—to delight in you
      every day.*
I vow to love all of you with all of me, forever and forever.

This time, my words matched my feelings. There was no disconnect between my insides and outsides. The noise was gone, replaced with a quiet certainty that I'd found my way home.

You're perfect together, John's mom said when we all hugged at the end. *Soulmates*, my mom added.

What a moment. What a *true* story.

The *D*-Word

WHEN THINGS GET HEATED BETWEEN JOHN AND me, it tends to look something like this:

John is disappointed and frustrated because he doesn't feel considered or heard. When he feels this way, I tend to get hyper-defensive because I hear that I'm a disappointment, I'm not good enough, and I'm failing him in the relationship. Rather than hear him out, I tell him that he's "making a big deal out of nothing" and begin to list off reasons why I'm not "bad" and why he is wrong. This only intensifies his frustration, so he doubles down on his point and speaks more sharply, trying to feel understood. I then point out his sharpness and make him wrong for it. Meanwhile, my mind races with the fear that he might leave me. My solution? I'll abandon him before he abandons me. While in reality he's just annoyed and wants to express it—my history tells me that since I messed up, he's not sticking around.

One night, a few weeks after getting married, one of these fights ensued. As much as I search my memory now, I cannot recall how the fight started or what it was about. But rarely was *what* we were fighting about the issue. It was *how* we fought.

In this particular fight, I threw a pillow. Slammed a door. Raised my voice. Shed some tears. And used my best fighting words. It was not my finest moment.

At one point I screamed, "I don't think we're compatible! This is over! I'm annulling our marriage! I want a divorce!" I waited, expecting John to match my level of intensity. But this time, he looked at me differently. He didn't raise his voice. He paused for a few moments and took me in—me in all my anger and fear and mess and pillow throwing. A smile spread slowly across his face, and then . . . he began to laugh.

"Why are you laughing?" I said, taken aback. "Nothing about this is funny!"

But he just kept laughing.

The rumble of his laughter broke me from my trance. *You're doing that thing you do. You're running when you think someone is going to run from you.*

Time slowed as I realized that I didn't need to protect myself from being left anymore. I didn't need to run away when I felt afraid. I am loved and I am lovable not in spite of my imperfections and messiness, but because of them. I can stop taking John's attempt at expressing his feelings personally, and I can choose a new response.

A smile stretched across my face. I started to laugh too. "Oh my god, I'm being crazy," I said, falling to the floor.

"Craaaazy," John said back.

"Hey!" I said, getting up and leaping on the couch next to him.

We laughed until tears were streaming down our faces.

"In all seriousness, though," he said, holding my hand tightly. "I do need you to stop threatening to leave when you're scared. It destabilizes the relationship."

"I know, I know," I said. "I'm really sorry."

"Let's make a final vow: We won't ever use the *d*-word—divorce. Real love can be hard and messy and chaotic—but we're partners through it all. Promise?"

"Promise."

It's two years later and that vow stuck. I never used the *d*-word again. Instead, I found the truth of what I was trying to say: *I'm noticing abandonment anxieties coming up for me right now, and that's making it hard for me to hear you. I want to be able to hear you, so I need a moment to step away from this conversation so I can catch my breath.*

One simple request turned chaos into connection.

This Just Works

JOHN WAKES ME BEFORE THE SUN HAS RISEN, kissing my face softly. "It's time to get up," he says, his voice warm and gentle. I slowly open one eye and see him smiling beside me. "Already?" I say, reaching out to pull him closer. "But what about morning cuddles?"

It's our two-year anniversary and we're off to Isla Holbox to celebrate—a small, car-free island north of Mexico's Yucatán Peninsula known for its turquoise waters, white sand beaches, and rich marine life. Our bags are packed, our meals for the day are prepared, and as per usual John is running ahead of schedule. He hates being late.

I get dressed and make our morning drinks while he finishes packing up our things. We turn off the lights, lock the door, and get in the car.

"Right on time," I say, and he smiles.

One Uber, flight, taxi, ferry, and golf cart ride later, we reach our destination: a boutique hotel on the edge of the island.

There's no cell service here, no TVs in the rooms, no distractions—just the warmth of each other's company. We drop our bags, leave our phones on the nightstands, and head to the bar for a celebratory drink.

Two mezcals—neat, please.

We take a seat at a table nestled against palm trees. The smell of copal incense fills the air. Waves sigh against the sand. It's too dark to see the beach, but my mind tries to imagine it. I turn toward John, look into his eyes, and reach for his hands.

"Two years," I say. "Thank you for choosing me and loving me the way you do."

"It's the great joy of my life," he says. "The most natural thing I've ever done. I couldn't not love you if I tried."

We touch our glasses. "Salud."

For hours, we sit there. There's no talk of work. I do not jot down strategies and next steps in my pocket-size notebook. I do not need to look at him beggingly to try to catch his eye. Instead I relish in how good it feels to be with someone who settles my nervous system.

At night's end we head back to our hotel room, four chocolate truffles and a card that says *Happy Anniversary* waiting for us. I shower, slip on my robe, and return to the bedroom to greet John. He looks at me with eyes that say *I want you.* I know how to look at him with eyes that say *I want you* now, so I don't have to try. He pulls me toward him and we embrace.

Then the kiss. The robe on the floor. The bed. I tune into my body, following what feels good. I listen to what his body says while hearing my own pleasure speak. There's no performance. No approval-seeking. No striving for perfectionism. I let myself come undone.

I curl into his body and rest my head on his chest, just as I do each night before sleep. He kisses my forehead and eyes and lips and says, "Good night, love of my life."

"Good night, love of my life," I say, my eyes closing, my heart smiling, my body surrendering into his. A chorus of crickets sings outside our room. *What a difference a few years makes,* I think.

Looking back, I can see the difference so clearly now. With my first marriage, I was always trying to fix what felt broken, filling the gaps with adventures, projects, and distractions, looking for the Thing that would save us. But it never came.

With John, there's no need to chase closeness or force connection or make anything happen. Loving him doesn't feel like work; it feels like breathing—effortless, natural, freeing.

In my first marriage, I told myself, *I can make this work.* With John, I don't have to tell myself anything. *This just works.*

Love-Able

FOR MOST OF MY LIFE, I BELIEVED BEING GOOD was the key to love and praise. If I was pleasing, perfect, agreeable—if I didn't disrupt the peace or make myself too much—then I'd be worthy of care and connection.

This belief shaped everything. I learned to read the room instead of myself, to measure my worth by how others responded to me. I mastered the art of approval-seeking, thinking love was something I had to earn. And for a while, it worked. Or so I thought.

But the cost was me.

I abandoned my truth to be agreeable, swallowed my needs to stay easy, and smoothed out my edges to fit into the version of myself I thought others would love. And even then, the love I received never felt like enough—because I never felt like enough.

My life changed when I realized this truth:

Being "good" wasn't the answer; being honest was. Going with the flow didn't bring me peace; it left me disconnected from myself.

I had to stop asking, *Who do they need me to be?* and start asking, *Who do I want me to be?*

217

This shift didn't happen overnight. It was awkward and messy, full of false starts and stumbles. But as I started to choose myself—to let go of perfection, to stand in my truth, to disappoint others rather than abandon myself—I began to feel something I'd been chasing all along: love, self-respect, peace.

Not the kind that comes from being good enough for someone else, but the kind that comes from being good enough for myself.

And the irony? Once I found that love within, the rest followed. The husband. The life. The joy. They weren't the source of my worth; they were the result of it. The real transformation wasn't about finding the right person or the right life. It was about finding myself.

It would be easy to stop the story here with a perfect bow. To tie it all up neatly, as if that's how healing works. But that's not how this story goes.

Because here's the truth: loving myself doesn't look how I thought it would. It's not a grand resolution or the final chapter neatly closed. It's a practice. A daily reckoning. A constant rewriting of the story I once believed about myself.

Some days I still want to hide from conflict or do whatever it takes to keep the peace. It still makes me uncomfortable when someone is disappointed in me. Some days I catch myself saying yes when I mean no, or feeling guilty for choosing what feels most true. Still I notice a desire to be liked when I walk into new rooms. And sometimes, I still compare myself to other women's perfectly curated lives on Instagram.

But the difference is this: Now I don't make it mean I'm

not worthy of love. Now I don't think I need to bend myself to fit someone else's expectations of me. I remind myself instead that love isn't something I have to chase, prove, or earn.

That's the story that stops here.

And just in time for a new one to begin.

Epilogue

Flames

Family dysfunction rolls down from generation to generation, like a fire in the woods, taking down everything in its path until one person in one generation has the courage to turn and face the flames. That person brings peace to their ancestors and spares the children that follow.

—*Terry Real*

I'M THIRTY-EIGHT YEARS OLD, IN AN OPERATING room, a sheet of fabric cutting my body in half. John is in scrubs, holding my hand. Classic rock is playing loudly, a team of doctors laughing, shouting, and moving around the room like it's their night out on the town. Besides a faint tugging sensation in my abdomen, the lower half of my body is numb. I'm about to meet my son through an emergency C-section. This is not how I thought this would go. But this is how it's going.

This time yesterday, contractions started in our home. John and I walked up a steep hill and through winding

220

neighborhood roads, holding each other through every surge. A few hours later, our doula arrived, and a few hours after that, the midwife. Everyone kept telling me the birth was going to be smooth—he'd slip right out. Our doula dreamt about it and my massage therapist said my hips were made for this moment. I hoped that'd be the case, but I've learned not to create expectations around things I can't control. When the time came for that final push, John wrapped his arms around me in a tub of warm water and I roared. But my son didn't come. We moved to the toilet, then the shower, then the birth stool. He still didn't come. After twenty-four hours of labor and five hours of pushing, John made the call: we're going to the hospital. As we'd soon find out, while his body was in the right position, his head was tilted back—he was stuck. Later my intuitive will tell me this is the sign of a strong-willed, independent soul who won't follow conventional norms; now knowing him, this rings true.

At 5:23 P.M., I heard my son cry for the first time. Doctors flurried around the room, cleaning him, weighing him, checking his vitals, John next to them with every step, singing *row, row, row your boat* to soothe his cries—the same song he sang when my son was in the womb. Minutes later, John placed him on my chest. Looking into my son's eyes, tears flowing, I said, "August, my love, I love you so much." He was quiet, still, alert—his eyes locked on mine.

I never knew what motherhood would feel like—I never even knew if I *wanted* to be a mother—but in this moment everything clicked. Why I left my marriage. Why I chose John. Why I chose me. Why I dove into the depths of my trauma, conditioning, and past. Why I was so steadfast in my need to heal and learn and grow and piece together my history. I think about meeting my father in that hospital room all those years ago, and how he was incapable of pointing his love toward me. I think about how I spent the next twenty-five years looking outward for that love. And now, as I look at my son, bare against my naked body, his warm breath against my chest, the full force of my love directed toward him and *only* him, it dawns on me:

I learned these lessons about love so he won't have to.

Everything I've done—every choice and every challenge— has led me to this. I get to teach my son to give and receive love freely—to stand tall in his truth and be fully himself no matter who the world tells him to be.

I don't want my son to be good; I want him to be free.

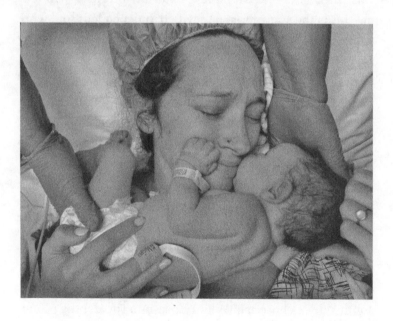

Acknowledgments

John: My deepest gratitude goes to you. Your support for me, in both my writing and my life, knows no bounds. The fact that you, an incredibly private person, encouraged the writing of this book means more than words can express. It is not lost on me that being a main character in someone else's story was never something you would have chosen, yet you gave me your blessing anyway because, as you said, "One should never get in the way of art." Thank you for encouraging me to leave you out of the writing process so I could write the book I needed to write, not the one I thought you'd enjoy. You know me (and my inner approval-seeker) so well. *I love you* is not enough.

I finished this book—final edits and all—six weeks postpartum. I wrote and rewrote in every spare second: during our son's naps, in the rocking chair in the middle of the night, and in the brief moments between caring for him. None of this would have been possible without you, John. You took on all the home responsibilities during this time, made my every meal, and even talked through edits with me when I was stuck. I know this wasn't always easy, but you never wavered. *Thank you* will never feel like enough.

Acknowledgments

Thank you to my therapist, Christine, for offering me the space, safety, and wisdom I needed to discover my truest self, and how to love her more deeply. If every person in the world had the privilege of working with a therapist such as yourself, the world would be a far more beautiful place.

Thank you to my agent, Sarah Passick. You're the best agent in the world. I can't believe you read every draft of this book—multiple times. Your encouragement and support and no-bullshit feedback mean the world. There's no one else I want to do books with.

Thank you to my editor, Joel Fotinos. You are the truest fairy godfather. You saw what this book was *really* about before I did, and your feedback was essential in helping me figure out how to tell this story. Thank you, thank you, thank you.

Thank you to Jeff and Chantel Goins for your support and guidance in getting the first draft down. This book wouldn't have become what it is without you.

Thank you to Juliane "Sparklepony" Bergmann for getting into the weeds of the story with me, asking the questions no one else asked, and encouraging me to trust my own voice and instincts in finishing the final draft.

Mom, thank you for all the ways you've shown me love, and all the sacrifices you made to support me. I know that parts of this book are difficult for you to read, and I'm grateful for your encouragement nonetheless. Your presence in my life has shaped so much of who I am, and I'm grateful for the full range of what we've experienced together.

Gram, thank you for being the warmest blanket, and a safe place to land, for all these years. I love you so much.

To my dear ones: Erin Claire, Vienna Pharaon, Laura

Acknowledgments

Lombardi, Erin Berman, Allie Mahler, Majo Molfino, and Emily Chong. You're the best friends a woman could ask for. Not only did you live this experience alongside me, but your wisdom and perspective made all the difference.

Thank you to my teacher (and our officiant) George Haas. Your breadth of knowledge is a treasure; your willingness and capacity to share it is the most generous of gifts.

Thank you to the NUSHU community and every woman there. I'm especially grateful to Vanessa Cornell, Ally Bogard, Yasmine Cheyenne, Nicole Whiting, Britt Frank, Erika Bloom, Audrey Wisch, Carly Lynn, Minaa B, Rebekah Borucki, and Chloe Harrouche. I shared this story aloud with you for the first time, and the way you hollered and squealed as I told it gave me the reassurance I hadn't known I needed.

Thank you to my On The Page writing community. It was an honor guiding you to write your most honest and true stories, and it was a gift to write my own alongside you.

Thank you to the entire St. Martin's Essentials team—I am overjoyed to be working with you. Thank you, Emily Anderson, for keeping everything on schedule and on track, even with all my requests for extra time. And thank you, Olga Grlic, for the beautiful book cover design.

About the Author

AMBER RAE (@heyamberrae) is a bestselling author and speaker best known for the books *Choose Wonder Over Worry* and *The Answers Are Within You*. She's also the creator of *The Feelings Journal*, a tool that transforms the way you engage with your emotions. Her writing and illustrations reach 9 million people per month, and her work has been featured in publications such as *The New York Times*, *New York, Today, Self, Fortune, Forbes,* and *Entrepreneur*. As a keynote speaker and teacher, Amber has worked with companies such as Kate Spade, Meta, Microsoft, and TED. Amber lives in New York with her husband and son.